MASTERING
MICROGREENS

HOW TO EASILY GROW NUTRITIOUS FOOD
365 DAYS A YEAR INDOORS

SUSAN PATTERSON
MASTER GARDENER

Disclaimer: All material on BackyardVitality.com and in this book is provided for your information only and may not be construed as medical advice or instruction. No action or inaction should be taken based solely on the contents of this information; instead, readers should consult appropriate health professionals on any matter relating to their health and well-being. If you think you may have a medical emergency, call your doctor or 911 immediately. The content of this book (text, graphics, and images) is not intended to be a substitute for professional medical advice, diagnosis, or treatment. Always seek the advice of your physician or other qualified health provider with any questions you may have regarding a medical condition. Never disregard professional medical advice or delay seeking it because of something you have read on BackyardVitality.com or in this book. The information and opinions expressed here are believed to be accurate, based on the best judgment available to the authors. Readers who fail to consult with appropriate health authorities assume the risk of any injuries. Reliance on any information and content provided by BackyardVitality.com and this book is solely at your own risk. In addition, the information and opinions expressed here do not necessarily reflect the views of every contributor to BackyardVitality.com. BackyardVitality.com acknowledges occasional differences in opinion and welcomes the exchange of different viewpoints. The publisher is not responsible for errors or omissions.

CONTENTS

The Joy of Microgreens 9

A Tiny Plant with Big Power 11

Sprouts, Shoots and Baby Greens and Mature Greens 13

Why Grow Microgreens? 15

Health Benefits 16

Microgreen Families 22

Ready, Set, Grow 23

Seeds 24

Trays, Flats and Other Containers 26

Growing Media 27

Light 31

Heat 34

Nutrients 34

Pre-soaking, pH Balancing and Watering 34

Sowing 38

Germination 38

Harvesting, Washing and Storing 39

Cleaning Up 42

Basic Growing Steps for Soil-based Growing 42

Basic Growing Steps for Hydroponic-based Growing 43

Tips for Success 44

Growing Microgreens for Profit 45

Common Microgreens 54

Arugula 55

Beets 57

Broccoli 59

Buckwheat 61

Cauliflower...63

Celery...65

Cilantro...67

Clover...69

Collards...71

Dill..73

Fennel...75

Genovese Basil..77

Kale...79

Kohlrabi...81

Mustard..83

Parsley..85

Pea Shoots...87

Purple Top White Globe Turnip..89

Radish...91

Red Acre Cabbage...93

Red Garnet Amaranth..95

Sorrel...97

Sunflower..99

Swiss Chard...101

Wheatgrass..103

Lesser Known Microgreens.. 105

Alfalfa...106

Anise...107

Barley..108

Borage..110

Brussel Sprouts...111

Carrot..112

Chervil...113

Chia..114

Chickpea...115

Chives...116

Chrysanthemum 117

Cress..118

Endive...119

Fava Beans 120

Fenugreek..121

Leek 122

Lettuce 123

Marigold..124

Nasturtium...125

Onion..126

Orach..127

Oregano...128

Popcorn 129

Quinoa..130

Tarragon 131

Frequently Asked Questions...**132**

Problem Solved 138

Yummy Recipes **142**

Greet The Sun Guacamole 143

Cheesy Spinach Pesto..145

Mushroom Microgreen Omelet...147

Savory Chickpea Pancakes 149

Lentil Tacos with a Kick 151

Sweet Potato Polenta and Egg 154

Smashed Chickpea Sandwich 157

Zesty Radish Microgreen Salad 159

Quinoa Microgreen Salad with Basil Vinaigrette 161

Lemon Arugula Pasta 164

Sweet Summer Seared Halibut 166

Special Sea Scallops 168

Easy Sheet Pan Fajitas 170

Green Machine Soup 172

Greek Salmon Burgers 174

Basil Strawberry Chocolate Tart 177

Tropical Twist Smoothie 180

Immune Boosting Power Smoothie 182

Minty Mango Green Juice 184

Zucchini Carrot Bread 186

Mint Chip Microgreen Popsicle 188

Happy Growing **190**

Sources and Studies **191**

THE JOY OF MICROGREENS

It has been an incredible joy to grow food for my family for over 20 years. Now that my children are all grown up and have established homes and gardens of their own, I have discovered ways to continue to reap an abundant harvest on a much smaller scale. Rather than being sad to abandon acres of gardens, I have embraced some new and exciting ways to continue to grow food in a manageable way, and I love every bit of it!

As a health coach, I know just how important plants are to overall health and wellness. One of my favorite ways to supercharge my diet is by eating microgreens. Microgreens are nothing short of miraculous. They are so tiny and such perfect representations of fresh, adult-size veggies, herbs, and greens. They have powerful and exciting flavors, and their nutritional value is way off the charts. Not only that, but they give any dish beautiful color and texture.

I have discovered just how easy it is to cultivate, harvest, and use microgreens. In fact, it is so easy and so much fun that I love to share it with others. I grow greens on my kitchen counter and anywhere I have a little extra space, which makes them super accessible and easy to care for all year round.

I love to toss a handful of tasty microgreens in my smoothies, soups, salads, or just eat them as a side dish with any meal. They are light, crisp, flavorful, and contain even more nutrients than their adult counterparts (more on this to come).

Someone asked me a while ago how to grow microgreens if they didn't have a green thumb. There is good news; microgreens are very forgiving plants and perfect for those looking to get started growing their own food. They take up little space and won't cramp your style with complicated care or special instructions.

Once you begin growing microgreens, you won't stop. Trust me. You will love the experience so much that soon you will be growing microgreens all the time. That is the beauty of these greens. You can supercharge your diet with this powerful superfood 365 days a year!

With the knowledge you gain from this book, you will be ready to begin growing microgreens and quickly advance to an expert level. The more you grow, the more you know. It is easy to become a microgreens farmer in no time and even have a solid home business growing micros.

It is my pleasure to introduce you to the wonderful world of microgreens. I know that you will find as much satisfaction in growing and eating micros as I do. Enjoy the journey through this book, where I share some exciting and inspiring information about these tiny, incredible plants and all they have to offer!

Susan Patterson, *Certified Health Coach and Master Gardener*

TINY PLANTS WITH BIG BENEFITS

First introduced to the California restaurant scene in the 1980s, a new and delicious trend has been sweeping the nation. Five-star chefs are using them in their best dishes, health enthusiasts are embracing their nutrient density, and now, more and more people who want to experience the joy of growing their own food and even making a profit from it are digging into growing their own microgreens (AKA micros).

Microgreens are mini plants, the seedlings of herbs, grains, legumes, and vegetables; miniature versions of full-size plants. To fully understand what microgreens are, we need to look at the stages of plant growth.

The first stage of plant growth of a seed is called a sprout. Next, as the sprout begins to grow, a baby plant emerges and is called a microgreen. In scientific terms, a microgreen is a plant that has fully developed embryonic leaves (also called cotyledon leaves), and the first sign of "true" leaves is visible. At this point, microgreens are generally about two to three inches tall.

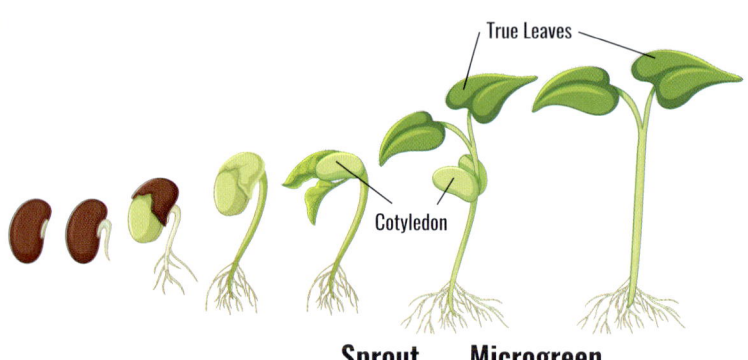

True Leaves

Cotyledon

Sprout **Microgreen**

Development Into The Microgreen Stage

Although there are many similarities between different microgreens, they vary widely in textures, colors, flavors, and health benefits. Depending on what plant they come from, the flavor of microgreens ranges from mild to tangy, spicy, or peppery. They may be small, but these hardy greens are easy to grow and pack a tremendous nutritional punch.

These tasty greens can be eaten independently but are often added to dishes for flavor and a serious health boost. Some common ways that microgreens are enjoyed are in soups, salads, smoothies, and juices. You will find delicious recipes and ways to use greens in this book, along with growing instructions and even how to start your own microgreens business for profit.

"Great things sometimes come in small bunches"

Sprouts, Shoots, Baby Greens, and Mature Greens

Before we dig too far into microgreens, it is essential to understand some terminology you may have heard before

What are sprouts? It may be that you have heard the terms sprouts and microgreens used interchangeably. However, as mentioned above, sprouts are similar to microgreens but not the same thing. The first difference comes in how each of these nutrient-dense foods is grown. Sprouts, known as the 'babies' of the plant world, germinate by being soaked or rinsed in water. They are the very first stage of visible plant growth when plants do not have leaves but have already germinated.

Sprouts and microgreens are harvested at different times. Sprouts are ready to harvest as soon as the seed sprouts out of its hull. This can take between 4 and 7 days. As mentioned earlier, micros are left to grow until they get their first set of true leaves. This can take from one to three weeks after the seed is sown.

Sprouts are eaten whole, root system intact, while micros are harvested by cutting the plant stem from the root.

What are shoots? Shoots are often confused with micros. In fact, shoots are just bigger microgreens. A good example would be a sunflower - they are often called shoots, not microgreens.

What are baby greens? Baby greens are another type of young plant that is harvested for nutritional benefit.

What are mature greens? Mature greens are leafy vegetables that you are probably most familiar with. These include plants like kale, spinach, and lettuce. These greens are grown to full maturity before they are harvested and eaten.

Microgreens carry a lower risk of foodborne illness than sprouts.

Why Grow Microgreens?

Here is a quick list of reasons why growing microgreens (micros) is an excellent idea. Whether you are a seasoned gardener or have never attempted to grow anything in your life, you'll fall in love with this tiny crop.

- Micros are quick to grow. Many types can be harvested in as little as eight days.

- Micros take up very little space. They have a very high yield to space ratio.

- Micros require minimal cost, time, and effort for a healthy harvest of greens.

- Micros are perfect for urban dwellers or those who have no time or space for a conventional garden.

- Micros only require a few things to be successful; good light, a shallow tray, water, and a growing medium.

- Micros can be grown all year indoors and in any climate.

- Micros are loaded with unique and intense flavors, textures, and living enzymes and nutrients.

- Micros come in a rainbow of colors and make an excellent garnish.

- Micros can be easily grown for profit.

Growing microgreens is a great way to teach kids about plants and gardening.

Health Benefits

Despite their small size and delicate appearance, microgreens offer substantial benefits beyond being an elegant garnish. They are indeed a valuable addition to any diet.

Microgreens contain high levels of:

- Phytonutrients
- Antioxidants
- Vitamins
- Minerals
- Enzymes

Although nutrient levels vary slightly depending on the variety, most microgreens are rich in potassium, iron, zinc, magnesium, and copper.

Microgreens are nutrient-dense

These tiny baby plants are loaded with nutrients. In fact, research shows that microgreens have a much higher concentration of nutrients than fully mature plants. As you probably know, most vegetables provide a wide array of nutrients. For instance, red cabbage is high in vitamin K and vitamin C, and kale is loaded with vitamin A and vitamin K, to name just a few. The micro versions of these plants are supercharged with the same vitamins - meaning you get more nutrients for your bite in the micro versions of the adult plants. With microgreens, you can easily boost your daily vitamin and mineral intake without having to eat full servings of adult veggies. In a study published in the Journal of Agricultural and Food Chemistry, microgreens were found to contain between four and 40 times more nutrients by weight than their fully-grown counterparts.

Microgreens contain phytonutrients

Micros come in a rainbow of colors that make your recipes deliciously bright and indicate the presence of phytochemicals, healthy plant compounds found in fruits and veggies. If you are a health-conscious person, you will know that eating a whole food diet loaded with colors is essential. Scientific studies confirm that colors signify great health benefits relating to phytochemicals in certain vegetables.

- **Green foods:** Excellent for energy, vitality, detoxification, and immunity.

- **Purple and blue foods:** Fight inflammation, promote youthfulness, and protect against certain types of cancer.

- **Red foods:** Can improve skin quality, reduce the risk of heart disease and diabetes, and help protect against certain types of cancer.

- **White and brown foods:** Boost heart health, bone health, and protect against certain types of cancer.

- **Yellow and orange foods:** Support healthy eyes and heart and improve immunity.

Microgreens contain polyphenols

Microgreens contain polyphenols, natural chemicals with protective antioxidant properties. Antioxidants are essential to help prevent the build-up of dangerous free radicals that can cause damage to cells and contribute to chronic diseases. Research shows that polyphenols can reduce the risk of heart disease, cancer, and Alzheimer's disease.

One study examined five micros from the Brassica family, including red cabbage, purple kohlrabi, mizuna, and red and purple mustard greens. The microgreens were found to be an excellent source of polyphenols and contained a wider variety of polyphenols than their mature vegetable counterparts.

Microgreens may improve heart health: There is no doubt; adding more vegetables to your diet is associated with a reduced risk of heart disease. Research shows that adding microgreens to your diet could help decrease certain heart disease risk factors, including obesity, bad cholesterol, and triglycerides.

"These data suggest that microgreens can modulate weight gain and cholesterol metabolism and may protect against CVD [cardiovascular disease] by preventing hypercholesterolemia."

Microgreens may reduce the risk of Alzheimer's disease: Research shows that foods rich in antioxidants, including those with a rich amount of polyphenols, may be linked to a lower risk of Alzheimer's disease.

Microgreens may reduce risk of diabetes: Antioxidants in microgreens may help reduce a particular type of stress that can prevent sugar from entering cells as it needs to. Studies have found that fenugreek microgreens can enhance sugar uptake into cells by 25-44 percent.

There is no difference between microgreen seed and regular seed, although certain varieties are better suited to growing as microgreens than others.

Microgreens may protect against certain cancers: Cancer causes uncontrolled cell growth. Research shows that eating enough of certain microgreens can suppress and even destroy cancer cells. This is mainly due to the phytonutrients present in these tiny green plants. The following are the top four microgreens that exhibited the ability to kill cancer cells in scientific studies:

- **Broccoli** - Broccoli contains a large amount of sulforaphane which has been shown to impact breast and prostate cancers positively. In one study, mice with invasive prostate cancer were fed broccoli microgreens for 12 weeks. Results showed an 11-fold reduction in invasive cancer cells.

- **Chickpea** - Peas and soybeans contain an anti-cancer compound known as isoflavones. In an in-vitro study, researchers from the *Chinese Academy of Sciences* extracted isoflavones from chickpea microgreens. They used these on breast cancer cells and found that they had a powerful inhibitory impact on the growth of cancer cells. Other in-vitro studies have found the same thing.

- **Rutabaga** - A 2013 human study from *Jagiellonian University* found promising results using eight-day-old rutabaga microgreen extract on human tumor cells.

- **Flax** - Researchers from *North Dakota University* have found that flax seed microgreens may induce cell death on breast cancer cells and slow down the cancer proliferation rate.

Microgreen Families

One of the greatest things about microgreens is the immense variety in flavor and texture that comes from the different plants. The most popular varieties come from these plant families.

- **Amaranthaceae family:** Includes amaranth, quinoa, swiss chard, beet, and spinach.

- **Amaryllidaceae family:** Includes garlic, onion, and leek.

- **Apiaceae family:** Includes dill, carrot, fennel, and celery.

- **Asteraceae family:** Includes lettuce, endive, chicory, and marigold.

- **Brassicaceae family:** Includes cauliflower, broccoli, cabbage, watercress, radish, and arugula

- **Cucurbitacease family:** Includes melon, cucumber, and squash.

- **Lamiaceae family:** Includes most common herbs like rosemary, oregano, basil, and mint.

- **Poaceae family:** Includes grasses and cereals such as barley, wheatgrass, corn, rice, and oats. It also includes legumes including beans, lentils, and chickpeas.

Arugula is one of the best microgreens for boosting immunity and helping maintain cholesterol levels.

READY, SET, GROW

With good light and adequate moisture, anyone can grow microgreens quickly from seeds. Although there are some variations when growing different types of microgreens, such as the best medium to grow in and blackout time, many things are similar, and if you are set up to grow one type, you can generally cultivate many others.

Microgreen terminology and important things to know

Before digging into the wide world of microgreens, it is important to understand some basic terminology and techniques for the greatest success. If you are new to microgreens, start with just one variety. The best choices for beginners include arugula, broccoli, kale, cabbage, chia, buckwheat, endive, mustard, and cauliflower. You can successfully grow a small tray or cup of microgreens in a warm and sunny windowsill. The best is direct sunlight from a south-facing window.

Seeds

There is nothing more essential to growing microgreens than starting with good seeds and understanding how to store them to maximize crop yield. If you start your microgreen journey with seeds that are unreliable, you will get frustrated quickly. A reliable seed company and fresh seed is a must!

Here are some things to keep in mind when choosing seeds.

- **Untreated and organic seed:** Always seek untreated and organic seeds. Keep in mind, all organic seeds are untreated, but not all untreated seeds are organic. Untreated seed has not been processed using any physical, biological, or chemical techniques before packaging.

- **Non-GMO seed:** Beware of genetically modified (GMO) seeds that have been injected with genes from another plant or animal to give them different traits. This could include features for frost tolerance, weed killer resistance, etc. Always purchase non-GMO seeds.

- **Heirloom seed:** Heirloom seeds have been passed on through time and are selected and saved because they have the best flavor and production in the home and small market gardens. When you choose heirloom seeds, you get the benefit of a long development cycle. Only the best tasting and most dependable varieties make the cut!

- **Hybrid seed:** A hybrid seed is created when two varieties of the same plant are crossed. Crossing involves taking pollen from the male flower of one plant and transferring it to the female flower of a different plant. The seeds contained in the female fruit will be hybrid. Hybrid varieties often have traits such as disease resistance, improved flavor, productivity, etc.

 Unlike vegetables that are frozen, preserved, and shipped for miles, microgreens should be consumed as soon as possible after harvest.

- **Date of harvest:** The date that seeds are harvested predicts longevity. Choose seeds that reveal the actual harvest date, not the date of packaging or expiration date.

Storing seeds

Most seeds do best when kept in an airtight container in a dark, cool location (between 55-70 degrees F) with less than 70% humidity. You can also maximize seed life by freezing, which will increase shelf life four to five times. If you use the best storing methods, your seeds should stay fresh for up to two years.

Trays, Flats, and Other Containers

Use any small, shallow, clean container. Disposable plates, plastic take-out dishes, and clear fruit or salad boxes work well. If you prefer, you can grow your microgreens on a tray. The tray should have holes on the bottom if you are using a soil-less or soil method. There is no need for holes if you are using a grow mat and a hydroponic method for growing. Some people use trays that are two inches deep when growing with soil to help support the greens a bit better.

Growing media

Media is basically what you grow your seeds in. Generally, growing media can be broken down into three primary categories.

Soil-based

Use a planting mix that drains well and is free of clumps. Because you harvest microgreens at one to three inches tall, it's not necessary to have many nutrients in the soil mix. Keep in mind that you want to keep the soil moist, but it can cause problems and hinder growth if it is too wet.

Soilless media

This type of media is composed of different non-soil mixes. Popular options include coco coir, blends of vermiculite or perlite with an organic amendment, or hydroponic lava rock. Many people prefer using soilless media because it is cleaner than soil media.

My Favorite Soilless Mix

2 parts screened compost
2 parts coco coir
1 part perlite

Mix and store in an airtight container.

Hydroponic

Growing microgreens using a hydroponic method is an easy option for beginners. The most basic system uses a grow pad that absorbs and retains water to keep germinating seeds and sprouts moist. Using a grow pad made from coconut coir, hemp, or other material also makes harvesting easier and cleaner.

More complex hydroponic systems may work better if you plan to grow a lot of microgreens. These systems include:

- **Wicking system** - This system uses a rope or felt wick to connect one container with water and nutrients and another container where the microgreens will grow. This system has no moving parts or pumps and is known as passive hydroponics.

- **Ebb and flow system** - This system, also known as a flood and drain system, uses a large container of nutrient-rich water located just below the growing trays. It uses a grow pad instead of soil. A timer attached to a pump floods the trays with nutrient-rich water several times a day, and the water drains back into the container. Because this system requires electricity, a power failure could result in crop damage.

- **Deep water culture system** - This system is best for large microgreen and vegetable grows. In deep water culture, plants are suspended above water, just the roots are in it. An air pump then oxygenates the water.

Advantages and disadvantages of soil growing

Many micro growers claim that growing in soil makes the greens taste better. Of course, this can be very subjective. It is easier to grow microgreens in soil and to set up and maintain growing systems using this medium. Starting out, using soil is also more cost-effective than hydroponic growing. There is some research supporting the fact that soil-grown micros are more nutrient-dense than those grown hydroponically.

Soil is not without its disadvantages as well. Topping the list is that micros grown in soil are dirtier than those grown in water. In addition, micros grown in soil may encounter problems with soilborne diseases and pests.

Advantages and disadvantages of hydroponic growing

Several crops do consistently better when grown in a hydroponic fashion. No soil is used when growing hydroponically, which means the growing process is less messy than a soil medium. If you plan to grow microgreens for profit, most customers, including high-end chefs, prefer them if grown hydroponically. This also makes taking a live tray of greens to the restaurant easier. Setting up a hydroponic system can be pricey, depending on how many trays of greens you wish to grow. Hydroponic systems can also encounter issues with mold. Furthermore, some crops just don't do well when grown hydroponically. The shelf life of water-grown micros can also be shorter than those grown in soil.

Note: Some types of microgreens should not be grown hydroponically. Large seeds should be grown in soil or soilless media, not a hydroponic system, because they prefer to be covered with a light layer of soil that allows for the seed coat to shed before the first set of leaves emerge. Examples of seeds that prefer soil are beets, chard, buckwheat, sorrel, sunflower, and peas.

Light

Optimal light is essential for success. Thankfully, it is pretty easy to achieve. If you have good sunlight where you are growing your micros, you may not need any supplemental light, but it is always good to have a backup light source. As much as microgreens need light - too much of a good thing can burn your tiny crops.

Microgreens require between four and eight hours of light daily.

Let's look at both natural and artificial light a little closer.

Natural sunlight

The best things about natural light are that it is free and natural. Plants, including microgreens, love natural light. However, natural light is not always available to people who live in colder climates. There is often not enough sunlight during the winter months for microgreens to be happy. Even in warmer areas, a few cloudy days can have a huge impact on micros. Microgreens require between four to eight hours of direct sunlight daily to perform their best.

Artificial light

The good news is that when natural sunlight is not enough, you can still grow microgreens. Artificial lighting is excellent for beginners because you have better control over the growing environment. For instance, you can place artificial lights on a timer so you don't have to remember to turn them on and off. One of the best things about artificial lighting is that you can grow micros anywhere - even in your dark basement!

Here are some popular artificial lighting choices.

- **Incandescent lights** - These light bulbs contain a thin wire filament heated by an electric current and emit a wide spectrum of light including ultraviolet and infrared light. Incandescent bulbs are not very cost-effective and use quite a bit of energy, which can cause a sharp rise in your electric bill.

- **Compact fluorescent lights** - These lights produce ultraviolet shortwave light. This type of lighting is a popular choice for microgreen growers as it gives off less heat than incandescent bulbs, uses less electricity, and lasts longer.

Put a tea towel over your seeds and place a weighted object on top. This helps your seeds anchor themselves in the growing media and grow strong. This works especially well for tall microgreens like sunflowers.

- **_Light-emitting diodes (LEDs)_** - This type of lighting produces low amounts of heat and is incredibly energy efficient. Although LED's are more expensive than fluorescent light, they tend to be more affordable in the long run. As a supplement to natural lighting, LED lights may be a good choicc; however, for a sole source, they are not effective for micros. Their narrow wavelengths don't mimic sunlight as well as a broader light spectrum. LED lighting can also make your microgreen growing area too warm, so it is vital to pay close attention when using it.

Note: Some micros require more light than others, so be sure to research your seed type before determining if you need an artificial light system. If you see that your crop is somewhat 'leggy,' that is a good indication that it needs more light. If you are growing your micros on racks, you will need supplemental light.

- **_Blackout_** - A microgreen blackout period is the amount of time in which microgreens need to be kept in the dark. A popular method to achieve this is to stack trays on top of each other. You can also use a tea towel to cover your seeds. Anything that reduces the amount of light reaching the seeds will do the trick. The duration of the blackout period depends on what type of seed you are growing, soil and air temperature, and moisture levels. It is recommended that you check your seeds after 48 hours to see if they have germinated. Some varieties such as radishes, turnips, broccoli, mustard, and kohlrabi only need 48 hours of blackout. In contrast, others like cilantro, celery, and borage need up to four to six days of blackout time.

Heat

Most micros prefer a room temperature of about 70 degrees F. Some, like cilantro, prefer soil temperatures a bit cooler. If your air temperatures are too low, you can use a grow or heat mat for supplemental warmth.

Nutrients

While you can be entirely successful growing micros in just water, many growers add some type of hydroponic nutrients to their water source. Choose organic if possible and follow product directions carefully.

Pre-soaking, pH Balancing and Watering

Some microgreens need to be pre-soaked before planting. If it is recommended that you soak your seeds, follow the exact duration of the soak period. Types of microgreens that should be pre-soaked include sunflowers, peas, beets, buckwheat, chard, and corn shoots.

Pre-soaking is not a difficult process.

- Start by measuring the amount of seeds you need and place them in a small strainer.

- Rinse the seeds to wash off any residue. Fill a bowl with water so that it is about one inch above the seeds.

- Cover the bowl with a lid or tea towel and place the seeds in a warm area for about 12 hours or overnight. Do not soak seeds any longer as they can begin to spoil.

- After soaking, drain off the water and wash seeds using a kitchen sprayer.

- Don't dry the seeds completely - you want enough moisture on them to prevent them from drying out.

- Place the seeds back in the soaking bowl and cover the bowl to let the seeds start to sprout. This will take 12 to 24 hours or until you see tiny sprouts bursting from the seed shell.

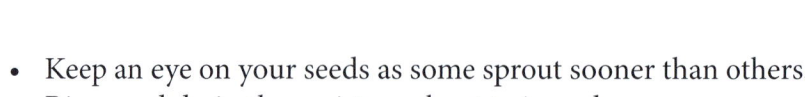

- Keep an eye on your seeds as some sprout sooner than others. Rinse and drain the moisture about twice a day.

- After about 36 to 48 hours from the first wetting of the seeds you should see tiny sprouts popping out. At this point, you can transfer them to the growing medium where they can continue to grow.

Seeds that float on top of the water when soaking are not viable and may not sprout

The ideal pH for microgreens

The ideal pH for microgreens is about 6.0. Most municipal water systems have a pH of around 7.0. Check your pH with a test kit (these are pretty cheap). To increase acidity, lower the pH levels by adding a little lemon juice to your water. To increase alkalinity, raise the pH levels by adding a small amount of baking soda to your water.

A good rule of thumb when watering microgreens is "keep them moist." A mister is a great way to accomplish this before germination. After germination, be sure to only water the soil, not the leaves, as this can encourage mold. When growing microgreens hydroponically, watering is easier. Simply lift the grow mat and put water on the tray up to the ridges. Watering this way will keep water from splashing on the micro leaves.

Microgreens are very resilient. If you forget to water, spray your soil or water as usual and watch your micros bounce right back.

Sowing

Different seeds like to be sown at different density levels, so it is important to know the best density for the seeds you intend to grow. For small seeds, use a rate of 10-12 seeds per square inch; for large seeds, a rate of six to eight seeds per square inch. Be careful not to plant seeds too thickly. This can result in a lack of air circulation and increase the risk of disease.

Germination

Germination time is sometimes called blackout time (mentioned above). This is the time where the seeds are establishing roots and getting ready to sprout. After a few days or so, you will see that the mini plants are growing. Once the stem reaches upwards, it is time to uncover your plants and let them soak in the light. The stem length is dependent on the type of microgreens that you are growing. For example, if you are growing sunflower microgreens, you can let the stems grow up to two inches before uncovering them. The stems will be yellow at first, but they will turn green once you expose them to the light due to photosynthesis.

Harvesting, Washing, and Storing

Failure to properly harvest, handle, and store microgreens can result in spoilage.

Harvesting

It is a good idea to know what your microgreens look like when they are mature. You should be able to look at your plants and know that it is time to harvest. With that said, the time to harvest is really up to you. You can harvest microgreens during the cotyledon stage (when the first two leaves or seed leaves appear) or during the true leaf stage.

Many microgreens taste best when harvested after the first leaves appear. However, any lettuce seed tastes best when harvested at the true leaf stage.

Taste your microgreens before harvesting. If you are new to growing, it is a good idea to keep a journal of how many days it has been since you planted your micros and how they taste. This will help you pinpoint the perfect time to harvest your microgreens. In short, the ideal time to harvest your microgreens is quite personal and varies depending on the exact taste you are going for.
Invest in a good pair of ceramic scissors. Ceramic is lighter, non-toxic, and chemically inert to the microgreens so that it will not transfer ions to the cut greens, which leads to faster oxidation and browning. Cut your micros just above the soil line or grow mat.

Some people like to clean their micros after harvesting. But, if there is no contamination of soil or seed hulls, you can simply snip with clean scissors and enjoy. If you plan on selling your micros, it is recommended that you wash them before packaging.

Rinse micros with cold water or fill your kitchen sink with cold water and soak micros to ensure that there is no soil left on them. It is important not to leave them wet if you plan on storing them. They will quickly go bad, even in the fridge.

A salad spinner followed by a gentle pat between two paper towels will get most of the water off your micros. You can also lay them on a screen where air can flow under and above. A fan will help speed up this process.

Storing

Microgreens can be stored in the fridge, but do not keep them in a sealed bag as they will spoil quickly. Circulation and moisture are important for storage. Lay a piece of wet paper towel in a container and cover the microgreens with another wet paper towel. Don't use a lid. Exposure to light while storing microgreens in the fridge can also accelerate deterioration.

If stored properly, microgreens will keep for a week or so in the fridge. Keep your fridge at about 40 degrees F and do not put micros in the freezer. Research shows that microgreens appropriately stored at 40 degrees F can last from 14 to 21 days, while those kept at 50 degrees F had a reduced shelf life of seven to 14 days.

Radish microgreens have the longest shelf life.

Opening and closing the fridge a lot can cause the temperature to fluctuate, so keep an eye on your micros. If you notice white spots, a bad smell, or sliminess when you touch them, it is time to throw them away. Eating microgreens that have gone bad can cause serious health issues.

Cleaning up

It is crucial to clean your scissors and trays before starting a new batch of micros. Never reuse any soil that has been used to grow microgreens. Throw it in your compost for later use in your garden. Soak empty trays for 10 minutes in a bleach solution of one tablespoon of bleach per gallon of water before using them again. Be sure that the solution makes contact with all parts of the tray. Alternatively, you can use a 35% food-grade hydrogen peroxide for sterilization.

Basic Growing Steps for Soil-based Growing

1   Poke a few small holes in the bottom of your container.

2   Cover the bottom of your container with an inch of moistened potting soil. Flatten it with your hand or a small piece of cardboard to remove any water pockets. Be careful not to over-compress.

3   Scatter the seeds evenly on top of the soil. Press them gently into the soil using your hand or a piece of cardboard.

4   Cover your container for blackout purposes.

5   Uncover and mist your seeds a couple of times a day.

6   Remove the cover and expose your microgreens to bright light after they have sprouted.

7   Water as needed.

8   Taste your microgreens as they mature and harvest when ready.

Use a clean spice bottle for even seed distribution

Basic Growing Steps for Hydroponic-based Growing

1   Pour one cup of water into your tray bottom (no holes).

2   Place your hydroponic mat in the tray and allow it to soak up the water.

3   Spread seed evenly over your mat. Keep in mind, the more seeds you spread on your mat, the denser your crop will be. Be careful not to let your seeds clump in one area.

4   Mist seeds thoroughly, cover, and place in an area at room temperature.

5   Uncover and mist your seeds a couple of times daily.

6   Once sprouts root, remove the cover and expose to light.

7   Water from the bottom as needed.

8   Taste your microgreens as they mature and harvest when ready.

Tips for Success

- Place your microgreens in a place where you will see them daily. This makes it easier to remember to water them.

- Although it is tempting to touch your micros, be careful not to over-handle the greens.

- If growing your micros in a sunny window, be sure to rotate them daily so that all parts get equal amounts of sunlight.

Can Any Plant be Grown as a Microgreen?

No. Some plants bear delicious fruit but have toxic leaves. This includes tomato and pepper plants as well as rhubarb.

GROWING MICROGREENS FOR PROFIT

If you are looking for a side business with a great ROI (return on investment), microgreens are for you. There has never been a better time to start your very own microgreens business.

Here's why:

- Microgreens are quickly gaining popularity not only amongst chefs but also the general public.

- There is an increased interest in buying fresh food locally.

- There are not many people growing microgreens, so the competition is relatively weak.

- Growing microgreens for profit is a great way to educate others about their amazing health benefits.

- There is an opportunity to start a subscription business that delivers to customers' homes. This produces a consistent, recurring stream of revenue.

- Microgreens return a higher profit per area compared to other locally grown produce.

How much can I earn selling microgreens?

Although there are variables to consider, growing a few types of microgreens can bring in about $20 per tray on average. If you invest about 20-30 minutes per day growing the greens, you make about $40 -$60/hour. Not a bad return on your time!

One of the best things about growing microgreens for profit is that it is a business that is easy to scale up by simply adding a few lights and equipment:

- One four-foot-wide shelf with two four-foot LED lights will give you eight trays per week (approx $160 profit)
- Two shelves will produce 16 trays per week (approx $320 profit)
- Four shelves will produce 32 trays a week (approx $640 profit)

The best thing is that even with four shelves, you only need a space of about 16 square feet. This makes growing microgreens for profit something most people can do, even with limited space and time.

How to get started

The first thing you should do is practice growing perfect microgreens. Get your lighting and watering down, your trays and equipment organized, and start small. Like I said, expanding your business and increasing yield is easy once you get the hang of growing.

Purchase the minimum supplies to produce eight flats a week with two types of popular seeds. As you make connections and fine-tune your marketing strategy, you can scale up.

Basic supplies needed

- *Lights* - Four feet of 6500k LED lights: Use two or three one-bulb fixtures per shelf. These can be purchased online.
- *Table* - You will need a table that will work for seeding, harvesting, and germination.
- *Grow rack* - When you first start, just hang a light over your work table. You can also purchase metal racks for under $100.
- *Growing medium* - Purchase high-quality potting soil or soiless grow mats.
- *Trays* - The best trays to purchase are 1020 trays with drainage holes.
- *Ceramic scissors* - Really sharp, clean scissors are best for harvesting.
- *Packaging* - Start with ziplock bags or use hinged plastic containers for a more professional look.

- **Fans** - Aeration is important when you are growing a lot of microgreens. Moving the air will help prevent disease. No need to purchase anything fancy for this; a simple fan will work fine.

- **Timer** - Putting your lights and fans on a timer helps automate your business.

- **Food-grade 5-gallon buckets with lids** - Purchase two buckets for soaking seeds.

- **Seed** - Purchase one to five pounds of easy-to-grow, popular varieties of seeds. The best are radish (Daikon, China Rose, and Rambo) and pea (Speckled). Purchase from a reputable company with high-quality seed. I like to use True Leaf Market for all seeds.

- **Scale** - Use this to measure your microgreens for packaging. A kitchen scale works well.

- **Mister and watering can with a fine spout** - As your microgreens grow, use the watering can to keep them moist.

Start your microgreen business for under $400!

Do your research

When deciding which marketing channel to explore, it is vital to take some time to research what is happening in your area and how well-serviced it is. This means going to farmer's markets, food co-ops, grocers, and restaurants to see what is available. If you find that microgreens are being sold in your area, be sure to visit the seller's website and find out what options they have available for customers to purchase their products.

Let's take a closer look at some of the selling avenues that may be available to you:

- **Grocery stores** - Stop in at your local grocers and ask them questions about their microgreen products and if they are happy with their current supplier. Grocers and co-ops are always looking for produce sources and may be especially interested in buying local. Keep in mind; your product will be fresh, which is an excellent marketing tool.

- **Farmers markets** - It is at farmer's markets that you may meet your most fierce competition. However, in most areas, microgreens are seriously underrepresented. Sellers often focus on mature crops, as these powerhouse greens are still fairly new to the market. Visit your local markets to scope out the competition and see how other sellers structure their prices.

- **Subscription sales (home delivery)** - The most untapped and profitable market for microgreens is a home delivery service. With a service such as this, you will be delivering microgreens to customers on a weekly, bi-weekly, or monthly basis. You can set up a website to handle subscription payments and allow buyers to select subscription options.

- **Restaurants** - If you live in a mid-size or bigger city, you will have access to several restaurants that may be interested in using microgreens in their menu. Make up a sample bag of your tastiest micros and deliver them to some local establishments during the slow part of the day. Include a price sheet and business card when you visit. When you sell to restaurants, you can charge a higher price than national distributors as your greens have the benefit of being locally grown. Your micros will be fresher. Plus, chefs love to support local farmers and advertise it for positive press. If you have a few good restaurant clients, you can make a fantastic profit. People who have twelve or more restaurant clients can sometimes earn a six-figure annual income!

Microgreens are sometimes called "vegetable confetti"

Find your niche

After you have done some research and determined what is happening on the local microgreen scene, it is time to find your own niche where you feel most comfortable selling your micros. Many micro businesses fall into one of three camps:

- Selling mostly main-commodity micros including radish, peas, sunflower, and brassicas.
- Selling special variety micros such as beets, corn shoots, cilantro, basil, mustards, and amaranth.
- Selling all types.

If you find that your local market is already saturated with people selling main commodity varieties, you may want to focus on specialty crops. If there is little competition in your area, you will likely be able to sell all types.

Popular microgreens for profit

Here are some of the most popular types of microgreens grown for profit.

- ***Radish*** - Both chefs and home cooks alike love radish for its pretty color and spicy flavor. You can choose green, purple, or mixed varieties.
- ***Peas*** - Peas are so easy to grow and give you an excellent yield. They also add wonderful texture variety.

- **Sunflower** - This popular micro can be a bit hard to grow and is usually grown by more experienced microgreen farmers.

- **Salad mix and broccoli** - Both salad mix and broccoli micros are popular as a health food and a bright garnish.

- **Curled cress** - This microgreen is used a lot in soups, salads, and sandwiches.

- **Beet, amaranth, and chard** - These microgreens add a brilliant splash of color to a dish but can be challenging. Like sunflowers, these micros are best suited for experienced growers.

 It is best to start small with only a few varieties and scale up from there

Packaging

Plastic containers with an airtight lid are best to keep micros fresh. If you deliver your micros for immediate use, domed plastic containers make a good impression on customers. This effect is compounded if you have a label you can put on the front with your company name and the name and weight of the container contents.

Records

Like any business, keeping records for each microgreen type you grow can be helpful for future growing. Your sheet should contain the following information:

- Seed variety and where you purchased your seed
- Date and length of time seeds were soaked
- Date and time trays were seeded
- Seed density per tray
- Growing medium
- Blackout time
- Growing conditions including lights, humidity, airflow, and watering
- Harvest date and time
- Yield
- Selling information, including price
- Customer information

COMMON MICROGREENS

In the vast world of microgreens, some are referred to as "common." Common does not always mean they are the easiest to grow, but simply the most popular and usual. This list comprises 21 of the most common microgreens.

Note: The seeding rates listed are for a standard 10x20" growing tray. Preferred growing mediums are listed. When you see soil listed, know that you can substitute a soil medium, if desired.

Arugula

Perhaps one of the easiest microgreens to grow, arugula is a popular choice for many recipes and microgreen mixes. In fact, it was the microgreen of choice in the 1980s when this urban gardening phenomenon first originated and was one of the first to pop up on gourmet restaurant menus on the west coast. Its bright green, heart-shaped leaves and unique texture make arugula the perfect garnish to finish off any meal.

Like the mature leaves, arugula microgreens have a sharp, peppery bite that gets less intense as the greens reach harvest time. Since it is one of the more potent microgreens, it is best in savory dishes that need a little flavor kick and is a great way to spice up a boring salad.

Common names: arugula, rocket, garden rocket, rocket salad, eruca, rucola, roquette, rugula, colewort

Presoak: No

Growing medium: Soil

Seedling rate: 1 oz

Blackout: 4-5 days

Germination time: 2-3 days

Time to harvest: 7-10 days

Health benefits

If you're not a fan of spinach but still want strong, healthy bones, arugula could be a great option. This nutrient-rich green is jam-packed with essential nutrients such as calcium and vitamin K, contributing to bone and muscle health.

How to use: Be sure to taste your arugula before adding it to your meals to determine the spice level and figure out what it will pair best with. It doesn't hold up well to cooking, so try to avoid heating it. Use it as a garnish for already-cooked food, in a salad, on sandwiches, or even in your green juice for a great detox and to wake up your sinuses.

Tips: Since the flavor changes as the greens grow, begin sampling them a few days before the expected harvest time and trim when they reach your desired flavor.

Beets

This microgreen boasts an interesting, earthy flavor that stands apart from other greens. It has dark green leaves, a red stem similar to the mature plant, and a rich nutrient profile. Detroit dark red beets and bulls blood beets are the most common microgreen varieties. Both have identical growing requirements; however, Detroit beets have a more wild growing pattern and aren't as straight as bulls blood beets, so keep that in mind when choosing your variety.

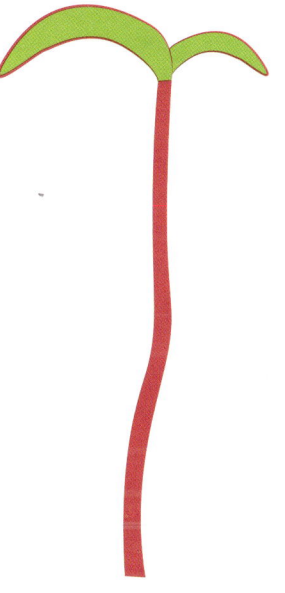

Common name: beets, beetroot

Presoak: Yes. 8-10 hours in cold water.

Growing medium: Soil

Seedling rate: 1.2 oz

Blackout: 5-6 days

Germination time: 3-4 days

Time to harvest: 12-15 days

Health benefits

With more iron per bite than spinach and a higher nutritional value than mature beets, these microgreens are a force to be reckoned with. They also contain high levels of vitamin K, which can help with blood clotting.

How to use: The bright red stem and green leaves make beets one of the most visually appealing microgreens. However, they do have a unique flavor that can make adding them to your meals a bit of a challenge. Use on top of toast with hummus or guacamole, or in scrambled eggs or an omelet to really let the red color pop against the yellow egg.

Tips: Beet seeds are slightly larger than other microgreen seeds so you may actually need to push them slightly into the soil instead of just scattering them on top.

Broccoli

Broccoli is in the cruciferous veggie family, which is well renowned for its cancer-fighting, antioxidant-rich vegetables. The microgreens of this popular plant are just as healthy and have a slightly bitter, cabbage-like taste that provides a fresh crunch when enjoyed raw. The leaves are a lovely, bright green, while the stems are a pale white, helping it stand out in a salad mix. This is one of the easiest microgreens to grow, making it the perfect choice for the beginner microgreen gardener.

Common name: broccoli, broccoli raab

Presoak: No

Growing medium: Soil

Seedling rate: 1 oz

Blackout: Yes. 4 days

Germination time: 1-2 days

Time to harvest: 7-10 days

Health benefits

Sulforaphane is a compound present in mature broccoli and microgreens. It can help fight and prevent lung and colon cancer and improve energy levels, complexion, digestion, mood, etc. This compound causes the slightly bitter taste of this veggie and gives it most of its potent health benefits.

How to use: Keep in mind, sulforaphane in microgreens is reduced when heated for too long at a high temperature. If you want to reap all of the benefits of this baby broccoli, be sure to enjoy it raw in smoothies or as a garnish. Like other microgreens, it can be mixed into a salad to change the flavor and complement your other veggies.

Tips: Since broccoli microgreens are so easy to grow, stagger the planting of a few trays so that you always have some fresh greens on hand. They are also incredibly versatile and can help protect against several chronic diseases, so adding a load of broccoli microgreens to your diet is a no-brainer. If you don't have room for many trays, try stacking one on top of the other while the bottom tray is in the blackout stage to utilize your counter or table space.

Buckwheat

This is a quick-to-mature microgreen that is perfect for growing with children who like to see results right away. Plus, the stems have subtle red and yellow hues that add interest and excitement. It is slightly tangy with a subtle sourness that really elevates the flavor profile and makes it a culinary goldmine for experimental dishes.

Common name: buckwheat, common buckwheat, Japanese buckwheat, silver hull buckwheat, lettuce buckwheat

Presoak: Yes. Overnight or for 8-10 hours in cold water.

Growing medium: Soil

Seedling rate: 12 oz

Blackout: 4-5 days

Germination time: 2-3 days

Time to harvest: 10-14 days

Health benefits

Like other microgreens, buckwheat is loaded with various vitamins, minerals, and compounds that improve your health and lower inflammation. However, there has been some concern expressed regarding increased skin sensitivity and irritation due to excessive buckwheat greens juice consumption and a substance known as fagopyrin. Keep in mind, too much of a good thing may be dangerous, so it is crucial to consume buckwheat microgreens in moderation to avoid any adverse effects.

Note: Don't juice this microgreen, as you often consume more greens than the daily recommended dose when you ingest them in liquid form.

How to use: Though buckwheat microgreens are delicious when added to other foods; they are especially delicious on their own as a snack. Simply harvest, rinse, remove any lingering seed shells, and enjoy munching on the flavorful greens.

Tips: Since the blackout time is longer than the germination time, the leaves may appear yellow at first. Don't worry! This is totally normal, and the microgreens are still safe to eat. The leaves will turn green once they are exposed to sunlight for a few days.

Cauliflower

Solid green, unassuming leaves with whitish stems and a pink and purple tint, the cauliflower microgreen is often forgotten in favor of the more flashy, spicy greens. However, this solid, easy grower is an excellent choice for the microgreen gardener looking for a salad base, as its mild taste will pair well with virtually any other veggies or microgreens. Don't underestimate the nutritional power of cauliflower! This tasty green is loaded with impressive health benefits.

Common name: cauliflower, snowball cauliflower

Presoak: No

Growing medium: Soil

Seedling rate: 1.5 oz

Blackout: 4-6 days

Germination time: 2-3 days

Time to harvest: 8-12 days

Health benefits

Cauliflower microgreens contain a group of substances known as glucosinolates (also found in other cruciferous veggies) that work in your body to prevent cancer and help protect cells from viral and inflammatory effects.

How to use: Since glucosinolates are degraded when exposed to heat, enjoy cauliflower greens raw or only slightly cooked to reap the optimal health benefits. Use in a salad or add for a few minutes to a hot skillet to sauté and enjoy as a side dish.

Tips: Unlike other microgreens, which tend to fall and become tangled with each other as they grow, cauliflower greens have an upright growing pattern and strong stalks that will keep them growing straight. This means that you can plant more seeds in a smaller area since you don't have to account for any sideways growth. It also makes it easier to harvest these seeds at separate times, as needed.

Celery

If you like celery, you'll love celery microgreens since they are basically a mini version of the mature vegetable. Unlike other microgreens, which have surprisingly distinct flavors and often taste nothing like the full-grown plant, you know what you are getting with celery greens. They have the same subtle yet sharp taste and crunch that is intrinsically tied to the juicy green stalks.

Common name: celery, turnip-rooted celery, celery root, knob celery, celery leaf

Presoak: No.

Growing medium: Hydroponic

Seedling rate: 0.75 oz

Blackout: 7-9 days

Germination time: 5-8 days

Time to harvest: 12-15 days

Health benefits

Every microgreen possesses extraordinary health benefits and celery is no exception. It is full of all of the typical vitamins and minerals, including vitamins A, K, C, potassium, and folate. However, one notable bonus of celery is that it is incredibly low on the glycemic index, which means that it has a slow, stabilizing effect on your blood sugar.

How to use: Avoid adding celery greens to heavy dishes, dips, or sauces or exposing them to intense heat, as this can cause the delicate leaves to wilt. Keep them to use as a garnish after cooking or to decorate drinks like a bloody mary. This green also pairs well with seafood and veggies such as carrots, parsnips, potatoes, and onions.

Tips: Celery varieties can vary widely regarding harvest and germination time, with some taking as long as three or four weeks before they are ready to eat. Be sure to consult your seed packet for more accurate information on your chosen variety.

Cilantro

Picture a piece of celery that has a tangy, orange-like taste, and you've pretty much captured the flavor of cilantro microgreens. Though these greens take a little longer to germinate and grow, the payoff is worth it. They have a bright flavor and emit a lovely aroma when you brush your hand over them.

Some people love the taste of cilantro, and some people hate it, claiming that it is "soapy" (blame genetics). If you fall into the former category, you'll undoubtedly enjoy the citrusy flavor of the baby greens and will love having them on hand to throw into your favorite recipes.

Common name: cilantro, coriander, Chinese parsley, Mexican parsley, slow bolt cilantro

Presoak: Yes. 4-6 hours

Growing medium: Soil

Seedling rate: 1.3 oz

Blackout: 6 days

Germination time: 4-6 days

Time to harvest: 14-18 days

Health benefits

Two carotenoids known as lutein and zeaxanthin are antioxidants located in the eye that can help filter harmful blue light wavelengths and keep the eye healthy while preventing macular degeneration and damage. The body does not produce these critical antioxidants, so it is essential to get them from dietary sources, including cilantro, which is loaded with these helpful carotenoids..

How to use: Since it tastes so similar to regular cilantro, it is easy to incorporate this flavorful microgreen into your meals. Use it in any Mexican-inspired meals with beans, corn, tomatoes, and a little lime juice or add to salsa or stir-fries to liven up any dish. It is also delicious in curry and guacamole or egg dishes with bell peppers.

Tips: Try to keep cilantro in a cooler environment (under 70 degrees F) as it won't thrive in warm weather. Remember, cilantro is one of the slowest growing microgreens. Patience is key! Some seeds will sprout quicker than others, so keep that in mind when waiting for your cilantro greens to appear.

To help prevent this and ensure even germination, place the seeds in a ziplock bag and roll over them with a rolling pin to release the seed and "crack" it. Then, add them to a fine mesh strainer and soak overnight before planting.

Clover

Though clover has a more mild flavor, it is anything but boring. This yummy microgreen is delightfully crunchy with a fresh, slightly sweet taste that complements savory dishes and balances out spiciness. When you harvest them, the younger they are, the sweeter they will taste, so avoid letting these microgreens grow past 10 days, or they will become bitter.

Common name: clover, red clover, crimson clover

Presoak: No

Growing medium: Hydroponic

Seedling rate: 1 oz

Blackout: 3-5 days

Germination time: 1-2 days

Time to harvest: 7-10 days

Health benefits

Clover isn't usually enjoyed in its mature form and is often viewed as a weed; however, this microgreen certainly has something to boast about regarding its nutritional value. It is simply bursting with magnesium, iron, zinc, calcium, and other surprising nutrients. Many people also recommend clover microgreens to help soothe various skin conditions such as eczema, psoriasis, and mild burns from the inside out.

How to use: Since clover doesn't have a potent flavor, it is an excellent addition to green smoothies or juice and is a great green to help you reach your vegetable quota for the day.

Tips: Clover usually has lingering seed hulls as it grows, so it may require vigorous rinsing after harvest to ensure that these are removed.

Collards

Though collards are often forgotten about, it is actually a very easy-to-grow microgreen that is perfect for beginners. With a similar flavor to the mature greens, collards microgreens may not be for everyone. In fact, there is some evidence to suggest that certain people are genetically predisposed to taste bitterness while others will enjoy a robust and hearty flavor.

It has bright green leaves with a light pink stem and is a perfect brassica green for hydroponic growing. However, it will also succeed in soil with proper care, so use whichever growing medium works. best for you.

Common name: collard, collard greens

Presoak: No

Growing medium: Hydroponics

Seedling rate: 1.2 oz

Blackout: 4-5 days

Germination time: 1-2 days

Time to harvest: 7-10 days

Health benefits

Collards are an excellent source of folate, which has been shown to play a significant role in the development of the fetus during pregnancy. It could help prevent neural tube defects and miscarriage, which makes it an excellent microgreen for pregnant women or those trying to conceive. It is also rich in dietary fiber to help improve digestion and prevent constipation.

How to use: To curb the bitterness of these microgreens, use them in dishes with plenty of real sea salt to help mellow them out a bit. Collards are also good when paired with creamy substances such as oil, butter, milk, and heavy cream, so incorporate them into any dairy-heavy recipes.

Tips: Use a slightly damp paper towel to pat away seed hulls once the microgreens have sprouted. This is an easy step that will save you a lot of hassle once harvest time rolls around.

Dill

Feathery leaves, a willowy stature, and a bright, tangy flavor mean that dill delivers just the right amount of flavor and flash without overpowering whatever it is added to. With a little care and attention, you can grow this forgiving microgreen right at home and enjoy it in just a few short weeks.

Common name: dill, dill seed
Presoak: No
Growing medium: Soil
Seedling rate: 1 oz
Blackout: 4 days
Germination time: 4-5 days
Time to harvest: 12-15 days

Health benefits

Dill microgreens could help manage diabetes, cholesterol, and metabolic syndrome. It can even benefit kidney disease, urinary tract disorders, and female reproductive health. Full of vitamins A and C, dill could also help reduce your risk of infection and shore up your immune system against disease.

How to use: Add dill microgreens to any dish with fish, eggs, or potato for a delightful flavor combination with lovely citrus undertones and a noticeable dill taste that enhances salt and other spices.

Tips: Due to their unique scent, dill microgreens may attract small insects that hover around the plant. These shouldn't cause any issue, but ensure that none linger after harvest by thoroughly rinsing the greens over a fine mesh strainer and spreading them out on a paper towel to dry.

Fennel

Not as potent as the mature bulb and fronds, fennel microgreen still has a noticeable licorice-like flavor similar to anise that you can easily incorporate into sweet or savory dishes. It is a delicate green that is tall and thin without a lot of crunch, making it a good choice for meals that already have that crunchy texture. Mild and clean tasting, fennel microgreens often look like blades of spring grass when mature, so try garnishing in small piles to enhance the visual effect.

Common name: fennel, fennel bulbs
Presoak: No
Growing medium: Soil
Seedling rate: 1 oz
Blackout: 3-4 days
Germination time: 2-3 days
Time to harvest: 10-14 days

Health benefits

Fennel microgreens contain nine essential amino acids that are critical for muscle health. The body cannot synthesize these amino acids, so getting them from food sources is essential to fix damaged tissue, help build muscle mass, and encourage your body to repair muscles following a strenuous workout.

How to use: Add to stocks, vinaigrettes, or toss on top of a salad with some feta cheese and a citrus dressing. These greens are also delicious in yogurt-based dips and make a flavor-packed pesto that is sure to please.

Tips: Fennel seed husks tend to stick around throughout the growing process and drop just before the plant is ready for harvest, so keeping an eye on those husks at the top of the sprout is an excellent indication of approaching harvest time.

Genovese Basil

One of the most popular herbs, basil makes an equally delicious and versatile microgreen. Though it takes a little longer to grow than other greens, the flavor is well worth the wait. Keep in mind; there are many varieties of basil microgreens that all differ in flavor, color, and texture, so it is crucial that you know what you are buying before you order seeds.

Genovese basil is one of the most popular since it is loaded with sweet flavor and packed with essential nutrients. It has a very similar taste to mature, sweet basil, which means that it can usually act as an adequate substitute in many recipes that call for this herb.

Common name: basil, sweet basil, great basil, Saint-Joseph's-wort

Presoak: No

Growing medium: Hydroponic or soil

Seedling rate: 0.7 oz

Blackout: Yes. 4-5 days

Germination time: 5-7 days

Time to harvest: 12-16 days

Health benefits

Citronellol and linalool are two essential natural chemicals in basil that give these tiny greens some serious anti-inflammatory powers. If you suffer from achy joints, chronic inflammation, or even arthritis, adding this microgreen to your diet could be a great way to bring back painless movement.

How to use: Use in any recipe that calls for basil or other Italian spices such as oregano or parsley. It is a very forgiving microgreen and won't dramatically alter the flavor of a dish but will add a nice depth and sweetness. It is excellent in pasta sauce, pesto, or pizza.

Tips: Basil seeds are mucilaginous, which means that the seeds will get sticky when wet and will often clump together. Take care while planting to ensure that the seeds will not be crowded. It is a good idea to add the seeds to a shaker bottle to help achieve proper spacing.

Kale

Many people hate the texture and taste of mature kale leaves, which is unfortunate, considering it is one of the most nutrient-dense foods per calorie. Thankfully, kale microgreens are equally nutritious but aren't nearly as bitter as the full-grown plant. The microgreens have a more mild taste, similar to romaine or red leaf lettuce, so you can enjoy large amounts in salads or smoothies without having to force yourself to get past the bitter flavor of mature kale. With dark green leaves and stems ranging from light purple to bright pink, these tiny greens are sure to add visual appeal to any dish as well.

Common name: kale, borecole, Tuscan cabbage/kale, Lacinato kale, curly kale

Presoak: No

Growing medium: Hydroponic

Seedling rate: 1 oz

Blackout: 4 days

Germination time: 2-3 days

Time to harvest: 6-10 days

Health benefits

Kale is often considered the most super of all the superfoods, and thankfully, these incredible benefits translate to the tender, less bitter microgreen. Mature kale is one of the best natural sources of vitamin K, which is critical for blood clotting and heart disease prevention. Kale microgreens are an even better source of this essential vitamin, with just one cup containing over ten times the daily recommended amount. The microgreens are also an excellent source of vitamin C, which can boost your immune system and keep you healthy throughout the cold and flu season.

How to use: Kale is one of the best microgreens for smoothies and juicing since it has a fairly mild flavor and blends in with other ingredients such as fruit or more potent greens.

Tips: Though it is a good idea to sow kale seeds densely to ensure a thick crop, be careful not to overseed as it can cause stunted growth and crop failure.

Kohlrabi

Kohlrabi isn't exactly a common household vegetable in the west; however, it makes an excellent microgreen. The name kohlrabi means "cabbage turnip" in German, a title that is certainly fitting for this cabbage-like root veggie. With a mild flavor similar to green cabbage or turnips, the microgreens can act as a chameleon in most dishes, subtly elevating the taste without changing it too much.

Lavender stems and light green leaves make this microgreen a favorite of gourmet chefs who often use it as a garnish to add a hint of color to dishes.

Common name: kohlrabi, German turnip, cabbage turnip

Presoak: No

Growing medium: Hydroponic

Seedling rate: 1 oz

Blackout: 3-4 days

Germination time: 2-5 days

Time to harvest: 8-12 days

Health benefits

Kohlrabi microgreens are full of vitamins and health-promoting compounds, including antioxidants which can help reduce diabetes, prevent cancer, and eliminate free radicals from your body. They are also loaded with potassium, a nutrient essential for keeping your muscles loose and your energy levels high.

How to use: Many people love adding kohlrabi to coleslaw since you don't have to slice anything, and it pairs really well with cabbage and carrots or other slaw ingredients. Serve this fresh, crunchy side with a light lemon or cracked black pepper vinaigrette for a delicious addition to any meal.

Tips: Kohlrabi is one of the easiest microgreens to grow and doesn't require much extra care or attention. However, the seeds are very dark, which makes them hard to see on the soil, and they are also round and somewhat bouncy, which can lead to them falling on the ground without you noticing. Be sure to pour the seeds on the tray carefully to avoid losing any.

Mustard

A fast-growing, snappy microgreen, mustard is the perfect choice for beginners but is still beloved by even the most experienced microgreen grower. While you will get some flavor variation depending on the variety you choose, most mustard micros have a spicy, slightly sweet flavor profile that isn't diminished even after cooking. Similar to radish, this green should be used primarily as a seasoning due to its intense, lingering taste.

Common name: mustard, mustard greens, black mustard seeds, yellow/white/brown mustard

Presoak: No

Growing medium: Soil

Seedling rate: 1 oz

Blackout: 3-4 days

Germination time: 3 days

Time to harvest: 7-10 days

Health benefits

According to studies, phenolic compounds are health-promoting phytochemicals with impressive antioxidant properties that are present in high amounts in mustard microgreens. Plus, mustard contains other vitamins that can help improve eye and heart health and keep your body running optimally.

How to use: One handful of mustard microgreens can change any dish entirely, turning a bland chicken breast, roast beef, or lackluster salad into a poetic expression of culinary arts. Get creative and experiment with your favorite meals by adding a sprinkling of this microgreen and taste-testing to see if you like it.

Once you understand the flavor (similar to horseradish), you'll become an expert at cooking with these delightful greens. Keep in mind; mustard greens also pair wonderfully with sushi, so feel free to top your takeout or make your own at home if you're feeling extra ambitious.

Tips: Mustard greens are fairly light-heavy, so be sure to use a grow light to prevent them from becoming leggy by reaching for the sun. There are many varieties of these greens with different colors and slightly different flavors, so read up on the types before placing an order.

Parsley

Though it takes longer to grow and germinate than most microgreens, parsley is surprisingly easy to grow and will do most of the work for you. After soaking, it has a high germination rate that increases your chances of a bountiful harvest.

It is a terrific garnish that delivers a mild parsley flavor, and its slightly curled leaves closely resemble mini versions of the full-grown herb. Use these greens anywhere you would typically enjoy parsley.

Common name: parsley, garden parsley, Italian parsley, curly parsley

Presoak: Yes. 4-8 hours in cold water

Growing medium: Soil

Seedling rate: 1 oz

Blackout: No

Germination time: 5-7 days

Time to harvest: 18-30 days

Health benefits

Rarely on any list of "all-time best health foods," parsley isn't always given the credit it deserves. Not only is it a favorite ingredient among chefs for its ability to dress up a meal, but it is a standout microgreen with notable health benefits. It can help promote circulation and heart health, improve liver function, and even help improve your immune system.

How to use: Cook these microgreens into any sauce, such as alfredo or tomato. Parsley pairs especially well with other Italian spices like oregano and basil, making these microgreens a perfect way to bring spaghetti night to a gourmet level. Snip off a few leaves whenever you need a handy garnish for virtually any dish or just want something to add a little greenery to the plate.

Tips: Since parsley microgreens take so long to mature, utilize succession planting to ensure that you will always have a fresh crop ready for harvest.

Pea Shoots

Even though peas require a few extra steps to get started, they grow with enthusiasm once they're in the soil and will send off attractive shoots and tendrils that make these some of the most exciting and visually appealing microgreens. The incredible flavor backs up the fascinating growth pattern, with a mildly sweet, fresh taste, crunchy texture, and adaptability to sweet or savory dishes.

Common name: peas, green peas, field peas

Presoak: Yes. 12-24 hours

Growing medium: Soil

Seedling rate: 12 oz

Blackout: 3-5 days

Germination time: 2-3 days

Time to harvest: 8-12 days

Health benefits

These microgreens boast seven times the vitamin C of berries and eight times the folic acid of the same amount of bean sprouts. They're jam-packed with fiber as well, which is essential for healthy digestion.

How to use: Add pea shoots to a strawberry-based salad with pecans, feta cheese, and vinaigrette to bulk up the greens and increase the veggie content. They're also delicious with any eggs or in Asian-inspired cuisine such as stir-fry.

Tips: When presoaking pea seeds, be sure to check the water level every few hours as the peas will absorb a lot of it and need to stay wet during this process. Following soaking, transfer seeds to a bowl or colander and mist lightly a few times every day until they begin to sprout. Finally, plant slightly sprouted seeds in the soil and continue with the blackout process. Mist once per day during the blackout to keep the soil damp.

Purple Top White Globe Turnip

Often an undervalued root veggie, turnips have a lot to offer regarding flavor, texture, and color. Though you might think it makes sense for turnip microgreens to taste like turnips, they actually have a flavor profile that is almost a combination of kale, spinach, and cabbage, though they are usually slightly sweeter. Often described as radish-like but without the spice associated with the red root vegetable, turnip microgreens have deep green leaves with whitish-pink stems.

Common name: turnip, white turnip, baby turnip, cabbage turnip

Presoak: No

Growing medium: Soil or hydroponic

Seedling rate: 1 oz

Blackout: 3-4 days

Germination time: 2-3 days

Time to harvest: 8-12 days

Health benefits

Turnip microgreens contain concentrated amounts of choline, an essential nutrient that can help protect cardiovascular and brain health, aid in relaxation, prevent insomnia, and even help with muscle movement.

How to use: Add to soups with other root vegetables such as carrots, potatoes, or radishes for a hint of green and a flavor enhancement or stir into your microgreen salad mix. You can also sautee the greens in a little bit of butter or coconut oil and top with a sprinkle of parmesan cheese for a yummy side dish or potato topping.

Tips: Turnip is easy to grow but prefers a lower light environment than most microgreens, so keep that in mind when choosing the location for your tray.

Radish

Like the mature veggie, radish microgreens are bursting with flavor, crunch, and spice, making them one of the most popular microgreens. They sprout quickly, don't require any special consideration for growing, and add the perfect punch to sandwiches and burgers. If something tastes good with a few radish slices, it will taste incredible with a handful of these yummy microgreens.

Common name: radish, daikon, white radish, icicle radish, Chinese daikon radish, Japanese radish, oriental radish, winter radish, Asian radish, Indian radish, giant white radish

Presoak: No.

Growing medium: Soil or Hydroponic

Seedling rate: 2 oz

Blackout: 3-4 days

Germination time: 1-2 days

Time to harvest: 6-12 days

Health benefits

Believe it or not, radish microgreens contain up to 40 times more nutrients than mature radishes. Think about it, all of the energy and nutrients that go into producing the red root vegetable you know and love are packed into a few bites of whole food goodness. According to a groundbreaking study, these nutrients include vitamin K, C, E, lutein, and beta-carotene, to name just a few.

How to use: Radish microgreens pair exceptionally well with fish, including salmon, tilapia, and halibut, and are an excellent topping for any grilled meat. These greens are also perfect for bulking up a sandwich and giving it that desirable crunch. Remember, radish is one of the more potent microgreens, so use it sparingly as a seasoning, not a base.

Tips: Harvest microgreens around day six for peak crunch and flavor. They will still be reasonably spicy when harvested later but will become leafier and not as succulent.

Red Acre Cabbage

These petite microgreens boast a yummy cabbage flavor with an additional hint of spice that the mature vegetable doesn't have. With violet stems and light green leaves, red acre cabbage microgreens are sure to impress when served with any dish. Take your average weekday meal to a gourmet level by incorporating these visually striking greens.

Common name: cabbage, red cabbage

Presoak: No

Growing medium: Soil or hydroponic

Seedling rate: 1 oz

Blackout: 3-5 days

Germination time: 2-3 days

Time to harvest: 5-14 days

Health benefits

Cabbage microgreens have long been lauded as an incredible health food. However, it is only recently that science has backed up these claims, with numerous studies showing that these tiny microgreens contain nearly 40 times the nutrient content of mature cabbage. Red cabbage microgreens have been proven to help reduce the risk of cardiovascular disease and even lower harmful cholesterol levels.

How to use: Since cabbage is a fairly delicate microgreen, it won't stand up well to cooking. Add it after cooking for interesting visual appeal or create a bed of attractive greens to serve fish or another main dish in style.

Tips: Add a thin layer of soil on top of the seeds after planting to help retain moisture and aid in germination.

Red Garnet Amaranth

This plant has been around for hundreds of years and was a staple in the diet of pre-Columbian Aztecs, who used it in many rituals and celebrations. In fact, it is estimated that amaranth made up about 80 percent of the food eaten by this ancient civilization. Unsurprisingly too, as it is easy to grow, versatile, and loaded with health benefits.

If you're looking for a striking microgreen that will really enhance the visual appeal of any dish, amaranth is the right choice. It is a vibrant pinkish-red color that stands out from other microgreens due to this natural, exotic hue.

It isn't just lovely to look at either; red garnet amaranth has a potent yet subtle flavor that is perfect if you like the taste of mustard microgreens but don't want as much spice. It is often described as nutty and slightly sweet, so it will pair beautifully with most dishes.

Common name: amaranthus, amaranth

Presoak: No

Growing medium: Soil

Seedling rate: 0.6 oz

Blackout: Yes. 4-5 days

Germination time: 2-3 days

Time to harvest: 8-10 days

Health benefits

You may have heard of amaranth referred to as a grain. In reality, it is a gluten-free pseudocereal, which separates it from traditional grains like oats and wheat. One of the most notable benefits of amaranth is its incredible protein content and vital amino acids.

How to use: Enjoy red garnet amaranth in any dish that looks a little bland. It is a perfect addition to green salads and is a great garnish for your homemade gourmet-inspired meals.

Tips: Amaranth is relatively sensitive to light, so the blackout time is critical. Be patient with this microgreen as it will take a little longer to sprout and won't grow as tall as other greens, so it will need to be harvested closer to the soil.

Sorrel

Unlike other microgreens that are often more spicy or mild and vegetable-tasting, sorrel has a bright, tangy, citrus flavor that sets it apart and makes it a must-have microgreen. Red-veined sorrel is the most popular variety of this unique green, boasting an attractive red stem that carries through the veins of the leaves.

Common name: sorrel, garden sorrel, red sorrel

Presoak: No

Growing medium: Soil

Seedling rate: 1 oz

Blackout: 3-4 days

Germination time: 5-7 days

Time to harvest: 12-20 days

Health benefits

Sorrel boasts an impressive nutritional content with several vitamins, minerals, and compounds that improve your health and well-being. It can even help boost your blood circulation due to its high potassium content.

How to use: Enjoy sorrel as a garnish on seafood, or mix it into rice with some chopped pineapple to give it a tropical flair that pairs well with shredded chicken or pork. It can enhance the flavor of any mild main dish and gives a little zing to smoothies or juices. Make a sorrel pesto to use on avocado toast, pasta, or sandwiches.

Tips: Growing sorrel microgreens requires a little bit of patience as they are slower to sprout and harvest than other microgreens. Stick with it, and you'll be rewarded with a bed of beautiful, tasty mini greens.

Sunflower

Along with arugula, sunflower is one of the most popular microgreens. With good reason, too! It is easy to grow, with a mild yet noticeable flavor, and it will sprout in just a few days. This is a great green to have on hand for virtually any salad or dish you can think of, as it will enhance the existing flavors and provide a nutty, earthy tone.

As a fun side note: Sunflower microgreens are commonly known as "sunnies."

Common name: black oil sunflower

Presoak: Yes. 8-12 hours

Growing medium: Soil

Seedling rate: 6 oz

Blackout: 3-4 days

Germination time: 1-2 days

Time to harvest: 8-12 days

Health benefits

Perhaps the most protein-rich microgreen, sunflower greens are a complete protein and contain a balanced supply of essential amino acids to help keep you full and aid in muscle tissue repair and proper enzymatic functions. They are also high in zinc which has been shown to help boost fertility in men, and folic acid, a necessary B-vitamin for pregnant women. You may want to add sunflower seeds to the menu if you plan to start a family soon.

How to use: This is the absolute best base for your microgreen salad. Whether you are going for a spicy salad with a bit of heat in the form of potent microgreens or peppers or want to land on the sweeter side and bring in some fresh fruit to top it off, this microgreen can serve as the backbone of your salad. It is also an incredibly delicious snack, made even better by the high nutrient content.

Tips: This is another light-heavy microgreen, so be sure to provide a direct source such as a grow light or place it close to a window. Also, don't forget the soaking step, as it is critical for encouraging germination and improving your chances of success.

Swiss Chard

In the same family as beets, swiss chard microgreens have a very similar flavor and color to their dark red cousins. They make beautiful garnishes and are perfect for the culinary artist who wants to create eye-catching and delicious food masterpieces. The pink stems contrasted with the light green leaves really make these greens pop.

Common name: Swiss chard

Presoak: Yes. 12-24 hours

Growing medium: Soil

Seedling rate: 2 oz

Blackout: 4-7 days

Germination time: 2-5 days

Time to harvest: 8-12 days

Health benefits

Kale and spinach are often seen as the most "super" of the greens, but swiss chard is hot on their tails. Not only does it have a large amount of antioxidants, but it is loaded with critical fiber, which can be essential for encouraging weight loss, stabilizing blood pressure, and maintaining a healthy glucose level in your blood.

How to use: Swiss chard has a fresh, slightly sweet flavor that enhances any microgreen salad since the flavor shines when this microgreen is eaten raw. Add it to a sautee of other fresh veggies with olive oil, garlic, lemon juice, and black pepper or sprinkle it over ground beef and serve over rice for a simple main dish that is perfect for a busy weeknight.

Tips: Like beets, try to cut swiss chard close to the soil to harvest the bright red stem. This may require a more vigorous rinsing to ensure that no dirt remains on the microgreens.

Wheatgrass

There's no other microgreen that resembles its mature counterpart quite as much as wheatgrass. Wheatgrass microgreen is just young grass that looks very similar to grass in your lawn. Don't let its unassuming appearance fool you, however, as wheatgrass is loaded with health benefits, and its rapid growth makes it a favorite microgreen for juicing. If you can look past a slight grass flavor and see all of the benefits beneath, you'll love having a tray of this green in your microgreen garden.

Common name: wheatgrass

Presoak: No

Growing medium: Soil

Seedling rate: 1-2 oz

Blackout: No

Germination time: 2-3 days

Time to harvest: 7-12 days

Health benefits

Wheatgrass has been extensively studied in recent years for its notable health profile as it has risen in popularity in the world of natural health and healing. Though it is often consumed in powder or supplement form, you can enjoy the same benefits by growing your very own wheatgrass microgreens in just a few days.

It is loaded with antioxidants, eight essential amino acids, and thylakoid, which can help with weight loss by reducing appetite. Wheatgrass has even been shown to reduce inflammation, particularly relating to ulcerative colitis, a disease connected to inflammation in the large intestine.

How to use: Though you can cook with wheatgrass, most people aren't exactly impressed by its rather bitter flavor. Instead, reap the benefits by adding it to a green juice with a flavorful ingredient like ginger, or simply juice pure wheatgrass, add a little water, and drink it like a shot.

Tips: Though the name might mislead you, wheatgrass is totally gluten-free, so you can enjoy it even if you have a gluten allergy..

LESSER-KNOWN MICROGREENS

If you are ready to take your microgreens experience to the next level, here are some lesser-known microgreens that you might want to consider.

Note: The seeding rates listed are for a standard 10x20" growing tray. Preferred growing mediums are listed. When you see soil listed, know that you can substitute a soil medium, if desired.

Alfalfa

There's nothing grassy about this delightful microgreen with large, deep green leaves and a mild cress-like flavor. It tastes delicious and is loaded with health benefits that could help reduce menopause symptoms, diabetes, and even prevent breast cancer. There's a reason that Alfalfa or "al-fac-facah" means "father of all foods" in Arabic.

Common names: alfalfa, lucerne, purple medic

Presoak: No

Growing medium: Hydroponic

Seedling rate: 1 oz

Blackout: 3-4 days

Germination time: 1-2 days

Time to harvest: 8-11

How to use: Alfalfa has a great crunch that makes it a wonderful addition to salads, sandwiches, and any other dish where it can be enjoyed raw. Serve it over fried rice to enhance the vegetable content and visual appeal of the meal.

Tips: Though some people have been concerned about lectin in alfalfa, which can prove toxic to humans, this compound is only present in the sprouting stage and decreases as the plant grows into a microgreen.

Anise

Round, bright-green leaves resemble those of parsley or cilantro. However, the flavor of anise stands completely alone. Anise microgreens are similar to their mature counterparts and boast a mild licorice flavor that works wonderfully in sweet dishes. This fragrant microgreen is also very popular for herbal remedies and tinctures.

Common names: anise, aniseed

Presoak: No

Growing medium: Soil

Seedling rate: 1 oz

Blackout: 3-4 days

Germination time: 7-10 days

Time to harvest: 12-20 days

How to use: Since it has a slightly sweet, licorice flavor, anise is one of the few microgreens that tastes best in sweet dishes. Use it to top off your ice cream, gelato, or frozen yogurt for a gourmet flare, or mix it into bread, cakes, and muffins for that delightful hint of licorice. Feel free to use anise microgreens in savory dishes as well, especially ones that would be enhanced by the unique flavor.

Tips: Some anise varieties will sprout quickly in about a week. In contrast, slow-growing varieties will take longer, so be sure to look at the seed packet for more information regarding the type you purchased.

Barley

If you have furry, four-legged friends in your house, you may want to grow this grassy microgreen just for them. Pets love chewing on barley leaves, and it is a great, safe alternative to lawn grass that can help improve their digestion and give them essential nutrients.

It is also a wonderful microgreen to juice and drink yourself. Though the flavor is often described as earthy or grassy, it is loaded with beneficial nutrients that make the slightly unappealing taste totally worth it.

Common names: barley, barley grass

Presoak: Yes

Growing medium: Soil

Seedling rate: 1 oz

Blackout: No

Germination time: 1-2 days

Time to harvest: 7-9 days

How to use: Unfortunately, cats and dogs will often have an instinct to chew on grass when let out in the yard, which isn't a problem on its own. But the grass in your lawn is often sprayed with toxic chemicals that can be harmful to pets if ingested. One way to avoid that is by growing a tray of barley microgreens for your pets for a green, nutritious snack.

When juicing for health benefits, try combining the barley with a piece of fresh ginger to add nutritional value and help mask the grassy flavor.

Tips: Since this microgreen is so easy to grow, try succession planting to keep a few trays on hand and ready to harvest. You don't have to worry about a blackout time and can cut the greens or let your pet chew on them after just one week.

Borage

Borage microgreens have a unique texture and flavor unlike any other. These light green microgreens have delicate hairs on the surface of the stem and explode with succulent juiciness when eaten. Borage boasts an intense melon or cucumber-like flavor that is delicious in soups or sandwiches.

Common names: borage
Presoak: No
Growing medium: Soil
Seedling rate: 0.7 oz

Blackout: 8 days
Germination time: 4-6 days
Time to harvest: 10-20 days

How to use: Though there may be a slightly bitter aftertaste to borage microgreens, they generally have a strong cucumber flavor that can be combined with virtually any dish. Incorporate into summer salads or fresh chicken sandwiches to mimic the flavor and crunch of cucumber.

Tips: Borage germination, blackout, and time to harvest are all a little longer than other microgreens. Stay patient and recognize that this yummy green won't sprout right away. You may also experience seeds germinating a few days apart from each other. If this happens, don't worry, you will still be able to grow a healthy crop.

Brussels Sprouts

With light green leaves and pink, purple, and white ombre stems, Brussels sprout microgreens are surprisingly attractive and add a nice, colorful element when used as a garnish. They taste similar to broccoli and cabbage microgreens with mild Brussels sprouts flavor and an edge of bitterness when the greens are enjoyed raw.

Common names: Brussel sprouts

Presoak: No

Growing medium: Soil

Seedling rate: 1.2 oz

Blackout: 3-4 days

Germination time: 2-3 days

Time to harvest: 7-10 days

How to use: Since Brussels sprouts are some of the prettier microgreens, they are an excellent garnish to top off salads or sprinkle over seared fish such as tilapia or halibut. If you're not a fan of the bitter aftertaste, cook them into dishes like tacos or shredded meat.

Tips: These microgreens prefer cool weather and may struggle in a warmer environment. Keep them away from hot windows that are exposed to direct sunlight.

Carrot

Carrot microgreens are very distinctive, with feathery tops that closely resemble the tops of the mature vegetable and look similar to dill, without the potent dill taste. Unlike full-grown carrot veggies, there's no orange root hiding under the soil; however, the delightful greens are reward enough. It is a neat-looking little microgreen that can be a good addition to salads with a very mild vegetable taste that doesn't change the flavor of whatever dish it is added to.

Common names: carrot

Presoak: No

Growing medium: Soil or hydroponic

Seedling rate: 1.3

Blackout: 4-5 days

Germination time: 4-7 days

Time to harvest: 14-20 days

How to use: Carrot microgreens are often utilized as fillers in various salads or as a garnish to enhance the visual appeal of a dish without altering the flavor. Throw them into any recipe that needs a bit of green or would taste good with a slight carroty flavor.

Tips: Germination and harvest time are slower than other microgreens, so don't be concerned if you don't see sprouts right away.

Chervil

If you want to enjoy the texture and taste of parsley but also want a microgreen with a little more flavor, grow chervil in your indoor garden today. This green has a mild parsley taste with a hint of anise or tarragon, making it a favorite among chefs and amateur microgreen enthusiasts.

Common names: chervil, curled chervil, French parsley, garden chervil

Presoak: No

Growing medium: Soil

Seedling rate: 1 oz

Blackout: 5-6 days

Germination time: 2-4 days

Time to harvest: 16-22 days

How to use: Chervil microgreens have a fresh, airy flavor that should be combined with a mild dish such as poultry, salad, or used as an attractive garnish. The leaves closely resemble parsley, which means that a single green can take your plate from drab to intriguing and appealing in just a few seconds.

Tips: Technically, chervil greens can be harvested as early as day 12, but letting them grow a little longer will ensure that you get maximum flavor and scent from this aromatic microgreen.

Chia

Chia seeds are a well-known superfood, beloved by many for their astonishing health benefits, high nutritional content, and unique water absorption capabilities. Chia microgreens are just as interesting and beneficial with a slightly minty, earthy flavor, meaning it is easy to include them in many meals. They help improve digestion and manage diabetes and are loaded with amino acids and protein, making these greens an excellent way to incorporate the benefits of chia seeds into a wide variety of dishes.

Common names: chia, chia seed, golden chia

Presoak: No

Growing medium: Hydroponic

Seedling rate: 1 oz

Blackout: 4-5

Germination time: 1-2 days

Time to harvest: 10-12 days

How to use: Chia microgreens are a perfect addition to smoothies since they won't absorb liquid and change the consistency of your drink like the seeds. You can also use them in salads or juices.

Tips: Since the seeds are mucilaginous, they will be covered with a gel-like coating when wet. They will start to clump together, so hydroponics may be an easier growing method to ensure proper seed distribution. Since the greens don't grow very tall, be sure to harvest close to the root.

Chickpea

Chickpea microgreens are an interesting white or light brown color that sets them apart from other greens. They are high in protein, iron, and calcium and have a pleasant flavor similar to a hazelnut. These greens are easy to grow and don't require blackout time, but you will want to keep a close eye on them during the soaking and germination periods and ensure proper spacing to prevent mold.

Common names: chickpea, garbanzo bean, bengal gram, Egyptian pea

Presoak: Yes. 1-2 hours

Growing medium: Soil

Seedling rate: 1 oz

Blackout: No

Germination time: 2-3 days

Time to harvest: 8-12 days

How to use: In an abundance of caution, it is best not to eat chickpea microgreens raw as they may be hard to digest. Steam them for a few minutes before eating to bring out the nutty flavor and ensure that you will still receive all of the vitamins and beneficial enzymes from the greens. Add a few spices and a pat of butter to the steamed greens and enjoy as a healthy side dish.

Tips: Be careful not to let the seeds soak for too long since the seeds are susceptible to molding with excessive exposure to water. The seeds can also become floury during germination, which can lead to breakage and mold. Plant immediately after soaking and cover with a light layer of soil to help avoid issues during germination.

Chives

Though chives are considered a more challenging microgreen to grow, their onion flavor is totally worth it. Instead of growing mature onions in the ground and waiting months to harvest, plant a few trays of chives and use them to add a noticeable flavor to any dish that calls for onions or garlic. They are slightly sweet, with a unique taste that sets them apart from other microgreens.

Common names: chives, Chinese chives, garlic chives, rock chives

Presoak: No

Growing medium: Soil

Seedling rate: 2 oz

Blackout: No

Germination time: 6-9 days

Time to harvest: 12-24 days

How to use: Chives are delicious in pretty much any savory dish. Use as a topping on hamburgers, mix into soups or stews, or enjoy on sandwiches or toast.

Tips: Be patient during the germination and growing process, as chives take a while to sprout and harvest. Consider succession planting so that you always have a tray ready for harvest. Though chives have a high germination rate, soaking them for a few hours may help increase your chances of success and speed up growth.

Chrysanthemum

The mature greens of this flowering plant are commonly used in Asian cuisine; however, the bitter flavor often turns many people away, and the greens usually have to be cooked to improve the flavor. On the other hand, the microgreens have a very similar taste without much bitterness and can be enjoyed raw or cooked. They lend succulent juiciness to any dish, and the lacy, serrated leaves elevate the visual presentation of your food..

Common names: garland daisy, chop suey greens

Presoak: No

Growing medium: Soil

Seedling rate: 1 oz

Blackout: 4-5 days

Germination time: 3-4 days

Time to harvest: 14-16 days

How to use: Use these pretty and delicious greens to add a grassy, pungent flavor to any dish. Enjoy them raw or lightly cooked in salads, on top of toast with smashed avocado and some sea salt, in hotpots, or sprinkled over tacos.

Tips: Combining chrysanthemum microgreens with lemon juice will help bring out the subtle lemon flavor of the greens and emphasize the sweetness while reducing some of the bitter edge. Remember, the blackout time could vary depending on the variety, so refer to the seed packet for more information.

Cress

Similar to mature watercress and mustard, cress is one of the most interesting microgreens from a flavor standpoint, with a strong, peppery taste that mellows as it matures. In fact, it is often agreed that cress is one of the most potent microgreens with a flavor unlike any other. Certainly a claim to fame for this unassuming green!

Common names: cress, garden cress, rock cress

Presoak: No

Growing medium: Soil

Seedling rate: 1 oz

Blackout: 4 days

Germination time: 1-2 days

Time to harvest: 8-12 days

How to use: Unlike other microgreens that can be used as lettuce for a salad base, cress has a potent taste that makes it more suitable as a spice or seasoning. If you want the strongest flavor, harvest at the beginning of the maturity window and use it right away. Cress is delicious in pretty much any dish that calls for black pepper, which means that it can be added to soups, combined with buttery potatoes for a flavor infusion, or even incorporated into your favorite meat recipe.

Tips: Be sure to keep moisture to a minimum when growing cress as it doesn't like to stay soggy and won't germinate or grow when overwatered. It is a mucilaginous seed, so it will develop a gel-like coating once you water it.

Endive

With its slightly bitter taste, endive certainly isn't for everyone. However, rather than an overpowering bitterness, it has a pleasant, mild flavor that combats natural sweetness or spiciness in salad mixes. It is a lovely, light green color that pops against darker meals, and once you get used to the taste, you'll enjoy pairing it with various food types for maximum flavor.

Common names: endive, chicory, frisée

Presoak: No

Growing medium: Hydroponic or soil

Seedling rate: 1 oz

Blackout: 3-4 days

Germination time: 2-3 days

Time to harvest: 7-12 days

How to use: Use this microgreen to add contrast to flavorful dishes. Any overpowering flavor such as salty, spicy, or sweet can be toned down and complemented by this dual-purpose green.

Tips: Endive grows wide and thick, not tall, so harvesting may be a little tricky. Cut as close to the soil as possible and rinse thoroughly to remove any dirt from the greens. Another way to avoid this issue is by growing it hydroponically since endive thrives in this growing system.

Fava Beans

Thicker and juicer than many microgreens, fava beans stand out in a salad and provide a noticeable crunch and earthy flavor. Fava bean microgreens have both the slight sweetness of peas and the nuttiness of sunflower microgreens and are a delightful treat.

Common names: fava, broad bean, fava bean, faba bean

Presoak: Yes. 12-24 hours

Growing medium: Soil

Seedling rate: 9 oz

Blackout: 4-5 days

Germination time: 3-4 days

Time to harvest: 12-15 days

How to use: Quite common in middle eastern cuisine, fava beans are a staple in many exotic recipes and dishes. They are perfect for stir-frying since they retain some of their crunch and don't get lost in the other veggies or soggy from the heat. Unlike other microgreens that are better raw, fava beans are even more delicious cooked and taste amazing when pan-fried with a squeeze of fresh lemon juice.

Tips: Fava beans sprout quickly and will grow thick and tall within a few weeks. Harvest earlier if you want a small microgreen, and let them grow a little longer if you want a standout, noticeable addition to your meal.

Fenugreek

Just like the seeds, fenugreek microgreens are commonly used in Indian cuisine to add spice, flavor, and just a little kick. They grow quickly and easily and are packed with essential nutrients and vitamins that can improve your overall health and wellbeing. The flavor is fresh and nutty with a mild spice and barely noticeable bitter aftertaste.

Common names: fenugreek

Presoak: Yes. 4-6 hours

Growing medium: Soil or hydroponic

Seedling rate: 0.6 oz

Blackout: 3-4 days

Germination time: 1-2 days

Time to harvest: 6-12 days

How to use: Add to a smoothie with a banana and cinnamon or sprinkle over a hummus and veggie sandwich. You can even prepare a refreshing detox cleansing tea by steeping fenugreek microgreens and fresh, sliced ginger in boiling water.

Tips: Be sure to soak seeds and water thoroughly when planting. Cover with a light layer of soil or a paper towel (if using hydroponics). This will help the seedling separate from the shell of the seed.

Leeks

Leeks have a delightfully strong sweet onion and garlic flavor that will elevate the taste of your home cooking and provide a fragrant aroma. The tall, thin greens will work well as an onion substitute. Just a few will go a long way, so be sure not to use too many as it can overpower a dish.

Common names: leek, wild leek

Presoak: No

Growing medium: Hydroponic

Seedling rate: 1 oz

Blackout: 3 days

Germination time: 3-4 days

Time to harvest: 10-12 days

How to use: Top hamburgers or sandwiches with leek microgreens or stir into vegetable or chicken soup. The flavor pairs well with virtually any savory dish.

Tips: Similar to chives, the seed hulls will stay on top of the leek microgreens, and the greens will be stems without true leaves. Don't worry; your microgreens will be ready to harvest around the 12-day mark. They just won't necessarily look like other baby greens.

Lettuce

There is an incredible list of lettuce varieties that grow wonderfully as microgreens. Most have a subtle, sweet lettuce taste similar to their mature counterparts with a white, red, or green stem and light green leaves.

Common names: lettuce, wild lettuce, Romaine lettuce, leaf lettuce, butterhead lettuce, round lettuce, head lettuce, iceberg lettuce, bibb lettuce, crisphead lettuce

Presoak: No

Growing medium: Soil

Seedling rate: 1 oz

Blackout: 4 days

Germination time: 2-3 days

Time to harvest: 10-16 days

How to use: The most obvious (and best) use of lettuce microgreens is as a salad base. Be sure to grow a few trays on rotating schedules so that you will always have some on hand. The mild lettuce taste means that you can easily incorporate more flavorful, potent microgreens. Use the baby greens to top sandwiches and burgers.

Tips: Lettuce microgreens are incredibly interesting because you can let them grow longer and harvest them as baby greens. Start tasting around the 10-day mark and harvest them anytime, letting them grow up to 21 days if you want to enjoy baby greens.

Marigold

Though many people think of marigold as just an ornamental flower, it is edible and can be enjoyed in its mature or microgreen form. The microgreen is green and has curled leaves and a light pink stem. It boasts a tangerine-like flavor with minty or spicy undertones (depending on the variety) and goes best with sweet dishes or cooked into baked goods such as bread and muffins.

Common names: marigold, gem marigold

Presoak: No

Growing medium: Soil

Seedling rate: 2 oz

Blackout: 3-4 days

Germination time: 2-4 days

Time to harvest: 8-14 days

How to use: Use marigold microgreens in baking to add a unique twist to your dessert or incorporate into mixed drinks or smoothies.

Tips: This is a super easy microgreen to grow. It is ready to harvest in about a week and doesn't require much extra care. Keep in mind; the flavor changes as the greens mature, becoming slightly less flavorful. Start trying the greens at one week and harvest when the desired flavor is reached.

Nasturtium

If you've never experienced the strong, wasabi-like taste of mature nasturtium leaves, you might be surprised by the potency of this unassuming microgreen. The lilly-pad style leaves closely resemble the mature plant, and the flavor is almost identical. Hot, intense, and delightfully spicy.

Common names: nasturtium, Indian cress, tropaeolum, garden nasturtium

Presoak: Yes. 4-6 hours

Growing medium: Soil

Seedling rate: 2 oz

Blackout: 3-4 days

Germination time: 4-7 days

Time to harvest: 8-12 days

How to use: The succulent stems and potent flavor make nasturtium microgreens perfect for stir-fries or other Chinese or Japanese-inspired dishes. Use anywhere you need a little extra kick. Naturistium microgreens are especially excellent when paired with sushi since they taste similar to wasabi.

Tips: Use warm water for the soaking process to help improve germination and cover with a light layer of soil after planting. Don't sow too thickly, as nasturtium greens can develop mold if crowded.

Onion

Like leeks and chives, onions taste almost exactly like the mature variety. Why even bother waiting for onions to grow when you can enjoy vibrant, flavor-packed microgreens after just two weeks? These greens usually have the seed hull attached at the top, but it can be rinsed off if desired.

Common names: onion, bulb onion, red onion, common onion, scallion

Presoak: Yes. 2-6 hours.

Growing medium: Soil

Seedling rate: 1 oz

Blackout: No

Germination time: 3-5 days

Time to harvest: 12-16 days

How to use: Use onion microgreens sparingly to add flavor where it is lacking. These greens are basically like tiny scallions and serve a very similar purpose in cooking. Top fried rice or shredded meat to increase the visual appeal and give your dish a finishing touch to round out the flavor profile.

Tips: Many people underestimate the intensity of onion microgreens. Be sure to taste a few to gauge the "onion-ness" before adding them to your food.

Orach

Purple or red orach are especially striking microgreens beloved by chefs for their incredible visual appeal. Deep purple or red leaves and stems with occasional light green spots and hot pink on the undersides of the leaves make these microgreens the star of any dish. Their slightly earthy and bitter taste is often compared to spinach, making orach an excellent microgreen to sprinkle over your plate as an attractive garnish.

Common names: orach, saltbushes, orache, purple orach, mountain spinach, red orach

Presoak: Yes. 8-12 hours.

Growing medium: Soil

Seedling rate: 2.5 oz

Blackout: 4 days

Germination time: 3-5 days

Time to harvest: 12-16 days

How to use: Orach is an excellent garnish since it doesn't necessarily have the most appealing flavor, but it has bold, red or purple-hued leaves that elevate your meal to a gourmet caliber. Serve a small portion on a bright, white plate and arrange a sprinkling of orach microgreens on top for the perfect display. You can also use it in any dish where you would use spinach, as it has a similar taste to the mature green.

Tips: Though soaking may increase the germination rate, some companies suggest that the seeds do not need to be soaked. Follow the instructions on the seed packet and grow a trial batch without soaking to determine if it is a necessary step.

Oregano

Oregano microgreens are excellent for adding flavor and Mediterranean or Italian flair to your meals. Use in bland dishes to add a unique, earthy tone or incorporate into familiar recipes to change things up and try something new. The stout, light green microgreens won't grow very tall, but they are loaded with flavor and sure to delight any palate.

Common names: oregano, origanum, wild marjoram, Common Italian Oregano

Presoak: No

Growing medium: Soil

Seedling rate: 1 oz

Blackout: No

Germination time: 5-7 days

Time to harvest: 16-22 days

How to use: Unlike other microgreens that are best when enjoyed fresh, oregano can actually be dried and used as a spice. Add to any dish that would taste good with seasonings like basil or parsley. This microgreen goes well with tomatoes and is a perfect addition to a savory sauce or soup.

Tips: Oregano microgreens require a little extra patience as they take a long time to mature and germinate. However, since they can be dried and stored, one harvest will last a long time. This microgreen is primarily used as a seasoning, and a little goes a long way.

Popcorn

If you want to elevate your microgreen growing experience to a whole new level and grow something truly unique, it's time to tackle popcorn microgreens. Yes, you read that right. These yellow microgreens are unbelievably delicious, with such a sugary flavor that they taste almost artificial. Be sure to harvest exactly at seven days. It is important to harvest before the leaves start to develop and change the flavor.

Common names: corn, sweet corn, yellow popcorn

Presoak: Yes. 8 hours in cold water

Growing medium: Soil

Seedling rate: 12-16 oz

Blackout: Entire growing period

Germination time: 2-3 days

Time to harvest: 7 days

How to use: Temper a spicy dish with the seriously sweet popcorn microgreen by adding it after cooking. Heating this green will reduce its flavor, so it is best enjoyed as a snack or added to salads or sandwiches.

Tips: Popcorn shoots are unlike any other microgreen in that they should be grown in a dark area from planting to harvest. Exposure to sunlight will cause the sprouts to turn green, the flavor to become undesirable, and the leaves to become tough and fibrous, making them virtually inedible. Keep them in a closed-off area such as a cabinet or tote with a lid during the growing process to ensure success.

Quinoa

Quinoa is an excellent alternative to rice since it is loaded with nutrients and is perfect for those who follow a gluten-free diet or people who want to limit their intake of carbs. The microgreen is just as nutritious, containing the nine essential amino acids you need to survive and tons of dietary fiber. Quinoa microgreens have a mild, earthy taste that doesn't overpower other flavors.

Common names: quinoa, kinuwa, ivory quinoa, red quinoa

Presoak: Yes. 30 mins-1 hour

Growing medium: Soil

Seedling rate: 1 oz

Blackout: 3 days

Germination time: 1-2 days

Time to harvest: 7-12 days

How to use: Enjoy this microgreen on top of fried rice or pasta to enhance the dish's visual appeal without altering the taste. Be sure to wash the mature microgreens before eating to rinse off any final traces of saponins.

Tips: There is some concern regarding allergies since quinoa seeds contain a compound known as saponins, which could cause digestive upset. Wash and rinse well before sowing until no suds remain on the final rinse to help reduce the saponins content and make the greens easier to digest.

Tarragon

Tarragon microgreens are small and short with an interesting flavor and scent that can serve as a fantastic garnish or seasoning for various dishes. Use sparingly, as the sweet, licorice-like taste can be potent, and the microgreens taste equally strong, if not stronger, than the full-grown herb.

Common names: tarragon, French tarragon

Presoak: No

Growing medium: Soil

Seedling rate: 1 oz

Blackout: No

Germination time: 3-7 days

Time to harvest: 10-14 days

How to use: Use tarragon leaves to add a nice flavor to fish, meat, soups, and stews. It also tastes delicious with tomato and eggs, so add it to your omelets or use it to season your tomato sauce.

Tips: Though not one of the most popular microgreens, tarragon is delicious and deserves a tray in your collection. Try some of the greens to acquaint yourself with the flavor if you aren't familiar with tarragon before adding it to your food.

FREQUENTLY ASKED QUESTIONS

I am gluten intolerant, can I still eat microgreens?

Here's the good news. Seeds that contain gluten, such as barley and wheat, are gluten-free at the microgreen stage. This is because the gluten is in the seed, not in the plant.

Can I eat microgreens if I am on blood thinning medicine?

Because many microgreen types have high vitamin K levels (the vitamin that aids in blood clotting), large quantities may cause issues for people taking blood thinner medication. If you are taking this type of medication, it is best to speak with your physician before consuming micros.

Do microgreens regrow after cutting?

No, most microgreens will not regrow after harvest. However, if there is one healthy leaf left, the microgreen may survive and regrow. This is because the seedling will be able to continue photosynthesis with light. Growth will be slower and stunted. Second harvest microgreens often taste different, which is why most growers harvest once and start again with new seeds.

Are microgreens susceptible to disease?

If you follow sowing density rates and have good air ventilation, clean equipment and do not overwater, your microgreens will stay happy, healthy and disease-free.

Can I grow microgreens in my outdoor garden?

Just like veggies, microgreens can be grown in an outdoor garden. However, you will find that they grow slower than they do indoors. It is also much more challenging to provide a blackout period for your crops. In addition, microgreens grown outdoors are often not as tender and tasty as those grown in a more controlled environment inside.

Will pests bother microgreens?

Microgreens grown indoors are generally not at risk from pests. However, if grown outdoors, they can easily be threatened by several annoying bugs such as worms, flies, ants, and caterpillars who will gladly munch on their goodness. If you must grow micros outside, try using a row cover to protect the young greens from predators.

Do I have to fertilize microgreens?

Technically, microgreens only need sunlight and water, as they contain all that they need to sprout, grow, and survive. Some people do use a diluted fertilizer, but it is not a requirement for success.

Can microgreens help me lose weight?

Because micros are nutrient-dense and low in calories, they make an excellent weight-loss snack or meal addition. With one gram of fiber per ounce, micros can keep you feeling full for longer.

What do I do if my cat is eating my microgreens?

A curious cat may want to nibble on your greens, especially if you grow wheatgrass. In addition to growing a special tray of micros for your cat, try covering your growing tray with a clear humidity dome or moving your growing system to an area that your cat can't access.

Can I dehydrate microgreens?

Yes, microgreens can be dehydrated, and it is a good idea if you plan to use micros for seasoning. You can dehydrate micros in the same way that you do other veggies.

Will cooking microgreens destroy the nutrients?

Cooking will reduce the nutrient content slightly, but there are ways that you can cook micros to retain nutrients. A popular method is to stir fry micros for a few minutes.

Can I grow microgreens in a glass container?

Many people prefer to use something other than plastic to grow microgreens and stainless or glass is a good option. A 9x12" glass baking dish works well.

Can microgreens make me sick?

It is doubtful that you will get sick from eating raw micros that are grown safely, but eating unclean raw microgreens can cause issues. Here are some examples of foodborne infections that you can get from eating dirty microgreens:

- ***Escherichia coli (Bacteria)*** - This is one of the most common infections, with symptoms including abdominal cramping, watery diarrhea, bloody stools, fever, and more.

- ***Salmonella (Bacteria)*** - Symptoms include nausea, vomiting, fever, headache, and more.

- ***Listeria monocytogenes (Bacteria)*** - Symptoms include fever and diarrhea.

- ***Norovirus (Virus)*** - Symptoms may include fever, diarrhea, and vomiting.

Note: Growing micros with a hydroponic method and a grow mat is much cleaner than using soil and will create less risk of contamination and sickness. Be sure to give your micros a rinse before eating raw to be on the safe side. Furthermore, using high-quality seed, clean and healthy growing conditions, and proper practices will help keep your greens as safe as possible.

Some microgreens can naturally make you sick when consumed in excess.

These include:

- **Buckwheat** - Buckwheat is a fast-growing microgreen that contains a compound called fagopyrin. If eaten in large quantities, these compounds may cause your skin to burn, swell, and turn red. It can also cause skin to become sensitive to sunlight for a few days.

- **Alfalfa and quinoa** - Alfalfa is a popular microgreen that is often used raw in various dishes. This micro contains saponins, lectins, and the amino acid canavanine. These compounds are harmless in low amounts but can cause inflammation, diarrhea, bloating, indigestion, and even lupus-like symptoms when consumed in large quantities. Quinoa also contains saponins that can cause negative reactions.

Remove saponins

To remove saponins, soak seeds in water and rub them together until the soap-like suds become clear.

Problems Solved

Here are some problems that you might encounter while growing microgreens and some simple solutions to apply.

Slow germination

Most seeds take 2-3 days to germinate, while some will take a bit longer. Presoaking seeds will help speed up this process considerably. Soaking wakes seeds up from their dormant stage and prepares them for growing, and it can be incredibly helpful for certain seeds.

Microgreens are drooping over

If your microgreens are falling over, it is a good idea to check your seed density. Drooping microgreens is usually a sign that they are not sown densely enough, as microgreens like to rest on each other while they grow.

Uneven growth

If your microgreens are growing well on one side of the tray and shorter on the other side, it is usually because the tall side is getting more light than the shorter side. All seedlings will naturally grow towards the light. If this is happening to you, make sure that your entire tray has equal light or rotate the tray as needed to achieve even growth.

Weak, leggy, and yellow stems

Microgreens that appear to be weak and leggy may have spent too long in the dark. The longer they stretch for light, the weaker they become. Pay careful attention to the blackout period to keep this from happening. Yellow microgreens are normal in the blackout period since the chlorophyll in the leaves has not yet carried out photosynthesis. As soon as micros are placed in the light, they will begin to turn green. One exception is popcorn microgreens that are harvested while still yellow.

Is that mold?

Many new microgreen farmers are shocked when they think that their greens are growing mold. Root hair (seen below) is also called cilia and is a natural structure of the root. It helps to increase surface area and reaches down to the water. Sometimes it can be hard to tell the difference between mold and root hair.

Here are some things to look for.

- Root hairs are fuzzy, mold is like a spider web.
- Root hairs are not slimy, mold is.
- Root hairs have no odor, mold smells musty.
- Root hairs will disappear after rinsing and come back in a few hours, mold does not disappear after rinsing.
- Root hair is found on the root part, mold is located above the soil level or in between the microgreens.

What if it is mold?

Mold growth occurs when the environment is too damp, has poor airflow, bad lighting, or a combination of these things. When mold occurs, micros may become unhealthy and fall over.

Mold can multiply quickly and will stunt microgreen growth. In addition, eating micros that are contaminated with mold can harm your health and your business, if you are growing for profit.

DO NOT eat microgreens raw if you find mold anywhere on your tray. You don't have to throw them out, though, as most germs can be destroyed with high heat.

Fixing a soggy environment - While moisture is key to the survival of microgreens, it is also a breeding ground for all sorts of microbes. One big mistake that beginners make is to use containers or trays without holes. This becomes a problem when excess water can not be drained out.

Humidity issues - Mold likes humidity and grows freely in humid environments. It is crucial to control the moisture in growing areas to keep mold at bay. If you have an environment high in humidity, consider investing in a dehumidifier.

Ventilation issues - Fresh air can help keep humidity levels down and reduce mold problems. Proper ventilation in your growing space is critical to success. Consider a fan to keep air moving, but don't aim the fan directly on your trays.

Grow media issues - Choosing the right media is critical for avoiding mold growth. Although many micro farmers prefer to grow in soil, hydroponic or soilless growing can be cleaner and help prevent mold.

Solving the mold issue

There are numerous ways to get rid of mold. The most common way is to add 3% food-grade hydrogen peroxide to a spray bottle and mist trays where you see mold growth. Be sure to carefully and entirely get rid of any moldy growth to keep it from ruining the entire tray of micros. If you are unsure, throw out the batch and start again.

Here are some other ways to prevent mold growth:

- **Sanitize seed** - Not all mold is due to something external; it can also occur if seeds are contaminated. To avoid this, sanitize seeds before you plant them. Simply add a teaspoon of hydrogen peroxide into the water and let seeds soak for a couple of hours.

- **Don't overseed** - Overseeding can make a mold problem worse. Be sure to follow the right seed density for planting. This will vary depending on the seed type that you use.

- **Use high-quality seeds** - The higher the quality seeds you use, the less chance that you will have issues. Check for hybrid seeds that are resistant to mold, if necessary.

- **Check drainage** - Micros like to be moist but not soaked. As mentioned above, water from the bottom to help reduce the chance of soggy microgreens.

YUMMY RECIPES

While microgreens are delicious to snack on raw, there is an infinite number of ways to enjoy them. Try these delicious recipes and experience the unique flavors of microgreens while benefiting from their nutritional density.

GREET THE SUN GUACAMOLE

Servings: 4
Total time: 10 minutes

While traditional guacamole is certainly a delicious treat; there's something even more appealing about the nutty, spicy flavor that sunflower shoots and jalapenos bring to this easy-to-make dip. Enjoy it with your favorite tortilla chips or pita bread, or spread on toast with an egg for a perfect lunch or breakfast loaded with protein and healthy fat.

INGREDIENTS:

2 avocados

Juice of 1/2 lime

¼ tsp sea salt

⅔ cup sunflower microgreens, roughly chopped

¼ cup red onion, finely chopped

½ jalapeno, finely chopped

INSTRUCTIONS:

1 Add avocados to a medium-size bowl and mash it with a fork or potato masher.

2 Stir in lime juice and salt until well combined.

3 Add sunflower shoots, red onion, and jalapeno into the bowl.

4 Refrigerate for up to three days in an airtight container.

5 Enjoy!

CHEESY SPINACH PESTO

Servings: 6
Total time: 15 minutes

The possibilities are pretty much endless when it comes to pesto. Use it on pasta, sandwiches, add a little vinegar to make it into a salad dressing, or mix it into rice or quinoa for a serious flavor upgrade.

INGREDIENTS:

½ cup pine nuts

2 cups spinach leaves, stems removed

2 cups arugula microgreens

2 cloves garlic, minced

¾ cup olive oil

¼ cup gruyère, grated

¼ cup mild and creamy goat cheese

¼ cup parmesan, grated

Juice from 1/2 lemon

½ tsp salt

¼ tsp pepper

INSTRUCTIONS:

1 Add the pine nuts to a skillet over medium heat and toast until fragrant and lightly browned.

2 Immediately add nuts and remaining ingredients to a food processor or high-powered blender and pulse until smooth or when it reaches your desired consistency if you prefer it a little chunky.

3 Taste test your pesto and adjust seasonings as needed.

4 Add to an airtight container and store for up to one week with a thin layer of oil on top of the pesto to keep it fresh.

MUSHROOM MICROGREEN OMELET

Servings: 1
Total time: 15 minutes

Eggs are a great way to start your day! Eating protein in the morning helps give you energy and keeps you motivated. This simple omelet can be cooked in just 15 minutes and will help you get to work on time with a full belly and a clear head. Don't forget the coffee, though!

INGREDIENTS:

1 tsp butter

3 eggs

½ Tbsp coconut oil

1 handful fresh microgreens, plus more for garnish

¼ pound mushrooms, sliced

Salt and pepper to taste

INSTRUCTIONS:

1 Heat skillet over medium-high heat and melt coconut oil.

2 Add mushrooms to the pan and cook until soft, about 4 minutes. Remove to a plate.

3 Whisk eggs, salt, and pepper together in a small bowl and melt butter in the hot skillet.

4 Add eggs to pan and cook for about 3 minutes, stirring until curds form and eggs are almost set.

5 Lightly flatten eggs into an even layer and add cooked mushrooms and microgreens to one half of the omlet.

6 Use a spatula to fold the omlet in half and cook one more minute to set.

7 Top with microgreens and salsa, if desired.

8 Enjoy immediately!

SAVORY CHICKPEA PANCAKES

Servings: 5
Total time: 20 minutes

These pea shoot chickpea pancakes make a delicious, hearty breakfast and are loaded with fiber and protein. Add your favorite savory toppings such as hummus, scrambled eggs, or salsa for a scrumptious, filling meal.

INGREDIENTS:

3 large eggs

1 cup cottage cheese

2 Tbsp olive oil

½ cup chickpea flour

1 garlic clove, minced

2 tsp lemon zest

½ tsp salt

1 cup pea shoots microgreens, chopped

3 Tbsp chives, finely chopped

INSTRUCTIONS:

1 Add cottage cheese, olive oil, chickpea flour, garlic, lemon zest, eggs, and salt to a high-powered blender or food processor. Blend until well combined and smooth.

2 Pulse in pea shoots and chives to roughly mix them into the batter.

3 Heat electric skillet to 350F or heat a large skillet on the stove over medium heat.

4 Add ¼ cup of batter for each pancake, cooking until bubbles form, about 2 or 3 minutes.

5 Flip and cook for another minute until the bottom is golden brown and pancakes are cooked through.

6 You may have to work in batches depending on the size of your skillet. Batter should make around 10 pancakes.

LENTIL TACOS WITH A KICK

Servings: 2
Total time: 30 minutes

Taco Tuesday never tasted this good. Take a break from meat and enjoy these vegetarian lentil tacos for the ultimate twist on your favorite dinner day of the week. Don't be afraid to adjust and personalize this recipe according to your preferences, as many of the ingredients can be omitted without changing the recipe. You can also add a tomato or sour cream, if desired.

INGREDIENTS:

¼ cup dried black lentils

1 cup vegetable broth

1 lime

¼ tsp cumin

¼ tsp coriander

⅛ tsp salt

1 cup microgreens

½ avocado

Minced chipotle in adobo sauce, adjust amount according to desired spice level

Honey

1 Tbsp olive oil

TOPPINGS (OPTIONAL)

Corn tortillas (for serving)

Sour cream

Salsa

Feta cheese

Cilantro, minced

INSTRUCTIONS:

1 Add lentils, broth, ½ lime, juiced, chipotle, salt, cumin, and coriander to a medium saucepan and cook over medium-high heat.

2 Bring to a boil and turn heat to low so that the mixture is reduced to a simmer.

3 Leave uncovered and cook for about 20 minutes or until lentils are soft and most of the liquid is absorbed.

4 While the mixture is cooking, dice avocado and add it to a bowl with microgreens of your choice.

5 Squeeze in juice from the other half of the lime, add a drizzle of honey to balance the spiciness, and mix in olive oil.

6 Toss until well combined and all ingredients are coated in the sauce.

7 Spoon lentils onto corn tortillas and top with a scoop of the microgreen mixture.

8 Add desired toppings. Feta cheese, cilantro and lime juice pair well with these veggie tacos.

SWEET POTATO POLENTA AND EGG

Servings: 2
Total time: 45 minutes

Sweet potatoes and naturally gluten-free polenta work together to create a tasty mash that will hit the spot on chilly winter mornings. Microgreens add crunch and spice to this otherwise mild dish, so be sure to include a flavorful green such as mustard or beet.

INGREDIENTS:

1 cup water

1 cup vegetable broth

½ cup dry polenta

1 large sweet potato

1 oz goat cheese

2 Tbsp coconut milk

Salt

2 eggs

Chili oil

Microgreens

INSTRUCTIONS:

1. Add vegetable broth to a medium-sized saucepan and bring to boil over medium-high heat.

2. Whisk in polenta, stirring constantly until it begins to thicken, about 3 minutes.

3. Reduce heat to a simmer, cover and cook for around 30 minutes, stirring occasionally.

4. While the polenta is cooking, set a pot of water to boil over medium high heat.

5. Peel and cube sweet potato and add to the boiling water.

6. Reduce heat to a rolling boil and cook until potatoes are fork tender, about 15 minutes.

7. Drain water and add to a large bowl.

8 Add goat cheese and milk to the sweet potatoes and mash until smooth. You can also use an electric hand mixer or blender if you desire a smoother consistency.

9 Once polenta is cooked, add it to the sweet potato mixture and stir until well combined.

10 Fry eggs in a skillet over medium-high heat.

11 Divide sweet potato polenta mixture into two bowls and top each with a fried egg, microgreens, and chili oil. Omit chili oil if you prefer a less spicy dish.

SMASHED CHICKPEA SANDWICH

Servings: 4
Total time: 15 minutes

In the heat of a summer afternoon, the last thing you want to do is slave away in front of a hot stove or oven for an hour, just trying to make a healthy lunch. Instead of grabbing for hormone-laden deli meat, try this fresh, vegetarian sandwich that will revolutionize your midday meal.

INGREDIENTS:

1 15 oz can chickpeas, drained and rinsed

½ lemon, juiced

½ cup red onion, finely chopped

1 tsp maple syrup

Kosher salt, to taste

½ tsp crushed red pepper

½ tsp coriander

½ cup English cucumber, chopped

2 Tbsp cilantro, chopped

Microgreens, for garnish

8 slices whole grain bread, toasted (use gluten-free bread, if desired)

Feta cheese for topping, if desired

INSTRUCTIONS:

1 Add chickpeas to a microwave-safe bowl and cook for about 3 minutes.

2 Mix in 2 Tbsp water, and lemon juice and smash heated chickpeas with the back of a fork until chickpeas stick together and form a chunky mash.

3 Stir in maple syrup, salt, red pepper, red onion, coriander, cucumber, and cilantro.

4 Toast bread in a toaster or toaster oven until lightly browned and crispy.

5 Divide chickpea mixture evenly among 4 slices of bread and top with microgreens for extra crunch and feta cheese, if using.

6 Add a second piece of bread on top and enjoy.

ZESTY RADISH MICROGREEN SALAD

Servings: 6
Prep time: 10

Whip up this super simple salad ahead of time and bring it with you for a perfect at-work lunch. It is easy to transport and will stay fresh for a few days. Simply wait to add the zesty lime dressing until just before you eat it for optimal flavor and texture. Use your favorite microgreen combinations to change the flavor and keep it interesting.

INGREDIENTS:

3 cups microgreens

6 radishes, halved or sliced

2 Tbsp lime juice

⅛ tsp dry mustard powder

¼ tsp salt

4 Tbsp olive oil

Coarse sea salt, to taste

Ground pepper, to taste

INSTRUCTIONS:

1 Add sliced radishes and microgreens to a bowl and toss until combined. Feel free to add other veggies or salad toppings, if desired.

2 Assemble dressing by combining remaining ingredients in a jar or salad dressing container and shaking to mix.

3 Store ingredients separately in the fridge for up to 4 days.

4 When ready to eat, simply shake the salad dressing and drizzle it over microgreens and radishes. Sprinkle with salt and pepper.

QUINOA MICROGREEN SALAD WITH BASIL VINAIGRETTE

Servings: 4
Total time: 30 minutes

You aren't limited to only including greens and other veggies in your salads. In fact, adding a few filling, protein-rich ingredients such as quinoa and black beans will keep you going throughout the afternoon and will help you avoid unhealthy snacking.

INGREDIENTS:

FOR THE SALAD:

1 cup uncooked quinoa

1 cup roma cherry tomatoes, halved

½ cup kalamata olives, pitted

2 ½ tbsp green onion, sliced thinly

1 14 oz can black beans, rinsed and cooked

½ avocado, cut into small squares

2 cups microgreens

FOR THE DRESSING:

2 cloves garlic

¼ cup red wine vinegar

¼ cup fresh basil leaves

1 tsp kosher salt

1 tsp black pepper

½ cup olive oil

INSTRUCTIONS:

1   Combine all dressing ingredients in a food processor or blender on high speed until liquified.

2   Slowly add oil while the blender is running.

3   Add to a jar and place dressing in the fridge while preparing other ingredients.

4   Cook quinoa according to package directions and let cool in the fridge.

5   Stir in remaining salad ingredients to the quinoa once cool and drizzle with dressing.

6   Quinoa salad can also be stored in the fridge for up to five days before eating so it is a great meal-prep option.

LEMON ARUGULA PASTA

Servings: 4
Total time: 20 minutes

This is an excellent gluten-free, veggie-filled alternative to traditional spaghetti or fettuccine alfredo. It is light, so it doesn't leave you feeling the need to take a nap after you finish your meal. The bright flavor notes of the lemon and basil will really elevate plain zucchini noodles, while the arugula microgreens provide a peppery twist.

INGREDIENTS:

6 medium zucchini

½ cup extra virgin olive oil

2 Tbsp butter

1 Tbsp garlic, minced

1 Tbsp lemon peel, grated

¼ cup fresh lemon juice

¼ cup vegetable broth

2 tsp dried basil

¼ tsp salt

⅛ tsp freshly ground pepper

1 cup arugula microgreens

½ cup chopped fresh parsley

Freshly grated
Parmigiano-reggiano

Sea salt

Freshly ground pepper

Squeeze of lemon

INSTRUCTIONS:

1 Using a spiralizer, prepare your zucchini noodles. You can heat them up slightly, but they will have better flavor and texture if left raw. Set aside.

2 Add oil and butter to a small saucepan over medium-low heat.

3 Once butter is melted, stir in garlic, lemon juice and peel, salt, pepper, broth, and basil and increase heat to bring mixture to a gentle boil.

4 Reduce heat to low and simmer for around 3 minutes.

5 Pour sauce over zucchini noodles and top with microgreens, parsley, grated Parmigiano-reggiano, squeeze of lemon juice, and salt and pepper.

6 Enjoy immediately.

SWEET SUMMER SEARED HALIBUT

Servings: 4
Total time: 50 minutes

This flaky halibut is seared to perfection and situated on a crunchy bed of microgreens for the optimal summer patio meal. Break out the string lights, cue some mood music, and invite your friends over for a classy outdoor dinner party featuring this sweet, salty, and scrumptious dish.

INGREDIENTS:

2 kiwi, peeled and diced

¼ English cucumber, diced

3 cups fresh strawberries, thinly sliced

Juice ½ lemon

1 Tbsp olive oil

Sea salt

Fresh ground black pepper

4 6-oz skinless halibut steaks, pin bones removed

¼ tsp ground cinnamon

⅛ tsp ground cayenne pepper

Coconut oil

⅓ cup torn fresh basil leaves, loosely packed

⅓ cup torn fresh mint leaves, loosely packed

6 cups assorted microgreens

INSTRUCTIONS:

1 Combine strawberries, kiwi, cucumber, lemon juice, olive oil, and salt and pepper in a large bowl. Cover and set aside. You can substitute any of these ingredients to personalize the recipe, if desired.

2 Mix cinnamon, cayenne, and salt and pepper together in a small dish and rub it over all sides of the halibut.

3 Melt a teaspoon of coconut oil in a skillet over medium-high heat.

4 Add halibut and cook for around 4 minutes on each side.

5 Fish should be flaky and slightly opaque with a golden-brown crust.

6 Divide microgreens among each plate and top with an even amount of strawberry mixture and one halibut steak.

SPECIAL SEA SCALLOPS

Servings: 4
Total time: 30 minutes

Impress your significant other with this perfect date night meal or save it for a special occasion to really "wow" them at the table. The seared scallops, microgreens, and lime miso sauce pair beautifully, but feel free to experiment with different sauces as you become familiar with the flavor undertones.

INGREDIENTS:

LIME AND MISO DRESSING:

3 Tbsp sweet white miso (be sure to get gluten-free, if needed)

2 tsp garlic, minced

1 Tbsp honey

1 Tbsp sesame oil

3 Tbsp fresh lime juice

1 tsp amino acids or soy sauce

3 Tbsp water

SEA SCALLOPS:

12 dry sea scallops, side muscles removed

Salt and freshly ground black pepper, to taste

2 cups microgreens

3 radishes, chopped

1 Tbsp coconut oil

INSTRUCTIONS:

1 To make the miso lime dressing, simply mix all of the ingredients together in a medium bowl until well combined. Store in the fridge in an airtight container until ready to use for up to one week.

2 Season the sea scallops on all sides with a pinch of both salt and pepper.

3 Melt coconut oil in a large skillet over medium-high heat and add scallops.

4 Cook for about 2 minutes per side until a nice golden-brown crust is formed and scallops are just opaque.

5 While scallops are cooking, combine microgreens, radish and 3 Tbsp miso lime dressing in a large bowl. Add more dressing, if desired.

6 Divide scallops onto 4 plates and add salad on top. Drizzle with extra dressing.

EASY SHEET PAN FAJITAS

Servings: 4
Total time: 30 minutes

Satisfy your craving for Mexican-inspired cuisine and amp up the heat with these easy, flavorful chickpea fajitas. Perfect for a busy weeknight, this yummy dish uses just one pan and takes under 30 minutes to throw together.

INGREDIENTS:

3 medium bell peppers (any color)

1 medium yellow onion

2 cups chickpeas, cooked

3 Tbsp olive oil

1 Tbsp chili powder

½ tsp garlic powder

¼ tsp cumin

1 tsp sea salt

8 corn tortillas

Fresh cilantro

Hot sauce, if desired

Microgreens

INSTRUCTIONS:

1 Preheat the oven to 450F. Line a sheet pan with parchment paper or a silicone baking sheet.

2 Slice peppers and onion into thin strips and place them in a large bowl.

3 Add cooked chickpeas.

4 Drizzle olive oil over chickpeas and veggies and sprinkle them with the spices. Toss to combine. Use a wooden spoon to ensure an even coating.

5 Spread out in a single layer on the prepared baking sheet.

6 Add to the preheated oven and cook for 20 minutes, stirring halfway through.

7 Serve alone or in corn tortillas with fresh cilantro and hot sauce, if desired.

GREEN MACHINE SOUP

Servings: 6
Total time: 40 minutes

Filling, warm, and flavorful roasted veggies create a delicate smoky flavor that gives this pureed soup something to brag about. Loaded with over two cups of microgreens and an entire head of broccoli, this hearty dish tastes delicious with a piece of crusty sourdough bread or alongside your favorite salad.

INGREDIENTS:

1 head broccoli,
cut into small florets

1 large yellow onion,
sliced into wedges

4 whole garlic cloves, peeled

1 Tbsp grapeseed oil

¼ tsp salt

4 cups vegetable broth

2 cups microgreens,
plus more for garnish

3 oz feta cheese,
plus more for garnish

1 cup cooked navy beans

Juice of ½ lemon

½ tsp chili powder,
omit if no spiciness is desired

TOPPINGS:

½ tsp chili powder

3 Tbsp roasted pumpkin seeds

Olive oil, for drizzling

INSTRUCTIONS:

1 Add a sheet pan to the oven and preheat it to 425F.

2 While it is preheating, chop broccoli and onion and add it to a large bowl. Toss together with garlic, grapeseed oil, and salt.

3 Remove the heated pan from the oven and spread broccoli mixture in an even layer.

4 Roast about 25 minutes or until broccoli is beginning to brown. Stir halfway through.

5 Add remaining soup ingredients and roasted veggies to a food processor or blender and blend until smooth. You may need to work in batches.

6 Rewarm in a large saucepan and serve with extra microgreens, feta, sunflower seeds, and olive oil drizzle.

GREEK SALMON BURGERS

Servings: 3
Total time: 35 minutes

You don't have to take a trip to an expensive gourmet restaurant to experience an exquisite meal. This dish is surprisingly simple and filled with fresh ingredients to enhance your palette and deliver essential nutrients. It has omega-3 fatty acid-rich salmon and a creamy, Greek-inspired sauce with the perfect amount of tang. Top with your favorite microgreens for crunch and a nice, spicy flavor addition.

INGREDIENTS:

SALMON BURGERS:

1 lb Sockeye salmon, skinned, pin bones removed

¼ cup onion, finely diced

¼ cup parsley or cilantro, finely chopped

2 ½ tsp sumac

2 tsp freshly squeezed lemon juice

2 tsp fresh thyme, chopped

1 egg

¼ cup gluten-free bread crumbs

Sea salt and freshly ground black pepper

1 Tbsp coconut oil

TZATZIKI SAUCE:

2 cups Greek yogurt

1 large cucumber

2 to 3 cloves of garlic, smashed to a paste

2 Tbsp fresh dill, finely chopped

1 Tbsp extra virgin olive oil

Fresh lemon juice, to taste

Sea salt, to taste

TOPPINGS:

Toasted brioche bun

Spring onion and radish microgreens

Tomato

Thinly sliced cucumber

INSTRUCTIONS:

1 To prepare tzatziki sauce, peel and grate the cucumber and use a paper towel or your hands to squeeze out excess moisture.

2 Combine grated cucumber in a medium bowl with yogurt, garlic, dill, olive oil, lemon juice, and salt to taste. Sample the sauce and adjust seasonings as desired. Refrigerate while you prepare the salmon burgers.

3 Roughly chop the raw salmon with a cleaver knife.

4 Add to a bowl and mix with remaining burger ingredients.

5 Use your hands to form 3, ⅓ lb burgers.

6 Melt coconut oil in a frying pan over medium-high heat and add burgers. Cook for 4 minutes. Flip and cook for 2 more minutes. Work in batches.

7 Add burgers to a toasted brioche bun and top with tzatziki sauce, a handful of microgreens, tomato, and thinly sliced cucumber pieces.

BASIL STRAWBERRY CHOCOLATE TART

Servings: 2
Total time: 55 minutes

If you're looking for a dessert that encapsulates all of the best things about summer and satisfies your love of chocolate without interfering with your clean eating goals, this otherworldly tart is for you. It is lightly sweetened by maple syrup, topped with sweet, clove-like basil microgreens, and a dollop of whipped goat cheese for a symphony of flavor.

INGREDIENTS:

CRUST:

1 cup almond flour

½ tsp salt

1 Tbsp cocoa powder

2 Tbsp maple syrup

¼ cup coconut oil, melted

FILLING:

1.5 oz goat cheese, room temperature

2 Tbsp Greek yogurt

1 Tbsp maple syrup

TOPPINGS:

1 ½ cups strawberries

Large handful of basil microgreens

INSTRUCTIONS:

1. To make the crust, whisk dry ingredients together in a bowl.

2. Stir in coconut oil and maple syrup until a crumbly dough is formed.

3. Divide the dough in half and press the crust into two mini pie pans, creating an even layer for your filling.

4. Pierce the dough with a fork a few times and place pie pans in the fridge for about 30 minutes.

5. While waiting, preheat the oven to 350F.

6. Bake for 15 minutes or until the crust just begins to brown.

7. Remove from the oven and let cool while preparing the filling.

8. Add filling ingredients to a high-speed blender and pulse to combine until smooth. Taste for sweetness and add more maple syrup, if needed.

9. Spread in an even layer onto crusts and top with strawberries and microgreens.

TROPICAL TWIST SMOOTHIE

Serves 1
Total time: 5 minutes

The natural sugar in the banana will help you gather the energy to start your day off right, while the coconut water and orange juice create a tropical taste that will transport you to a beach in the Caribbean. Choose a mild microgreen to get all of the nutrients without the "green" flavor that comes along with many microgreen smoothies.

INGREDIENTS:

¾ cup freshly squeezed
orange juice

¼ cup coconut water

1 frozen banana

⅓ cup Greek yogurt

1 cup microgreens

INSTRUCTIONS:

1 Blend all ingredients

2 Enjoy immediately!

IMMUNE-BOOSTING POWER SMOOTHIE

Servings: 1
Total time: 5 minutes

No matter how healthy you are, your immune system could always use a little help. This drink is sure to give it just the boost it needs to fend off colds and the flu and keep you feeling in tip-top shape. Plus, it has three different types of microgreens to help you use up your harvest.

INGREDIENTS:

½ cup pea shoots microgreens

⅛ cup oregano microgreens

½ cup radish microgreens

1 frozen banana

½ mango, cubed

1 cup freshly squeezed orange juice

½ cup plain yogurt

Squirt of honey

INSTRUCTIONS

1 Blend all ingredients

2 Enjoy immediately!

MINTY MANGO GREEN JUICE

Servings: 1
Total time: 10 minutes

Center your mind and body with this minty, slightly spicy green juice that will help deliver critical vitamins and minerals. Plus, it is absolutely delicious, so if you're not a fan of green juices, this is a great place to start!

INGREDIENTS:

½ cup mixed microgreens

6-8 large mint leaves

1 mango, peeled and
cut into chunks

1-inch piece of fresh ginger root,
peeled and chopped rough

1 lemon, juiced

5-6 coconut water ice cubes

Chia seeds, for garnish

INSTRUCTIONS:

1   Add all ingredients to a
high-powered blender and
blend until smooth.

2   Strain through a fine
sieve to remove pulp and
garnish with chia seeds.

ZUCCHINI CARROT BREAD

Servings: 6
Total time: 20 minutes

With just seven ingredients, these nutritious patties couldn't get any easier to make. Enjoy these with a little butter and salt anytime you want a savory snack. Who needs potato chips?

INGREDIENTS:

1 cup microgreens, roughly chopped

2 zucchini

2 large carrots

1 cup Parmesan cheese, grated

3 eggs

2 Tbsp chickpea flour

1 tsp garlic powder

INSTRUCTIONS:

1 Grate zucchini and carrots into a large bowl and mix in cheese and microgreens.

2 In a separate bowl, beat eggs and stir in flour, garlic powder, and salt and pepper.

3 Add egg mixture to veggies and stir to combine.

4 Flatten mixture into patties and cook in a lightly greased skillet for 4 minutes on each side.

5 Serve immediately.

MINT CHIP MICROGREEN POPSICLE

Servings: 6
Total time: 10 minutes

Mint, chocolate, and microgreens. Though it may seem like an unusual combination, you'll quickly change your mind once you taste these lightly sweetened, creamy popsicles that allow you to get your daily dose of microgreens in the most delicious, unexpected way possible.

INGREDIENTS:

1 can full fat coconut milk, room temperature

2 cups fresh mint leaves

20 drops liquid stevia

1 cup microgreens

Dash of cardamom

½ cup dark chocolate chips

INSTRUCTIONS:

1 Add chocolate chips to a high-powered blender or food processor and pulse until chopped to desired size. Remove to a small bowl.

2 Combine coconut milk, mint leaves, stevia, and microgreens in a blender until smooth and liquified. Add a little water to thin, if needed.

3 Mix in chocolate chip pieces and pour mixture into popsicle molds.

4 Add the sticks and freeze until hardened. Enjoy!

HAPPY GROWING

Now that you have the microgreen itch and see just how amazing these baby plants are, it is time to get growing. I wish you much happiness as you reap all the benefits of growing and eating these tiny yet powerful plants. Once you start growing micros, it will be hard to stop; they are tons of fun, packed with nutrients, and tasty too!

May all your micro gardens grow well!

Sources

Bazzano, Lydia A, et al. "Dietary Intake of Fruits and Vegetables and Risk of Cardiovascular Disease." *Current Atherosclerosis Reports*, U.S. National Library of Medicine, Nov. 2003, www.ncbi.nlm.nih.gov/pubmed/14525683.

Beaver, Laura M, et al. "Broccoli Sprouts Delay Prostate Cancer Formation and Decrease Prostate Cancer Severity with a Concurrent Decrease in HDAC3 Protein Expression in Transgenic Adenocarcinoma of the Mouse Prostate (TRAMP) Mice." *Current Developments in Nutrition*, Oxford University Press, 26 Dec. 2017, www.ncbi.nlm.nih.gov/pmc/articles/PMC6041877/.

Beaver, Laura M, et al. "Broccoli Sprouts Delay Prostate Cancer Formation and Decrease Prostate Cancer Severity with a Concurrent Decrease in HDAC3 Protein Expression in Transgenic Adenocarcinoma of the Mouse Prostate (TRAMP) Mice." *Current Developments in Nutrition*, Oxford University Press, 26 Dec. 2017, www.ncbi.nlm.nih.gov/pmc/articles/PMC6041877/.

Ben-Arye, E, et al. "Wheat Grass Juice in the Treatment of Active Distal Ulcerative Colitis: a Randomized Double-Blind Placebo-Controlled Trial." *Scandinavian Journal of Gastroenterology*, U.S. National Library of Medicine, Apr. 2002, www.ncbi.nlm.nih.gov/pubmed/11989836.

Chen, Hua, et al. "Isoflavones Extracted from Chickpea Cicer Arietinum L. Sprouts Induce Mitochondria-Dependent Apoptosis in Human Breast Cancer Cells." *Phytotherapy Research : PTR*, U.S. National Library of Medicine, Feb. 2015, www.ncbi.nlm.nih.gov/pubmed/25287332.

Dauchet, Luc, et al. "Fruit and Vegetable Consumption and Risk of Coronary Heart Disease: a Meta-Analysis of Cohort Studies." *The Journal of Nutrition*, U.S. National Library of Medicine, Oct. 2006, www.ncbi.nlm.nih.gov/pubmed/16988131.

Duchnowicz, Piotr, et al. "Effect of Polyphenols Extracts from Brassica Vegetables on Erythrocyte Membranes (in Vitro Study)." *Environmental Toxicology and Pharmacology*, Elsevier, 23 Sept. 2012, www.sciencedirect.com/science/article/pii/S1382668912001408.

Ebert, Andreas, et al. "(PDF) Amaranth Sprouts and Microgreens – a Homestead Vegetable Production Option to Enhance Food and Nutrition Security in the Rural-Urban Continuum." *ResearchGate*, 2015, www.researchgate.net/publication/272356648_Amaranth_sprouts_and_microgreens_-_a_homestead_vegetable_production_option_to_enhance_food_and_nutrition_security_in_the_rural-urban_continuum.

He, K, et al. "Changes in Intake of Fruits and Vegetables in Relation to Risk of Obesity and Weight Gain among Middle-Aged Women." *International Journal of Obesity and Related Metabolic Disorders : Journal of the International Association for the Study of Obesity*, U.S. National Library of Medicine, Dec. 2004, www.ncbi.nlm.nih.gov/pubmed/15467774.

Ishii, Satoshi, et al. "Anti-Inflammatory Effect of Buckwheat Sprouts in Lipopolysaccharide-Activated Human Colon Cancer Cells and Mice." *Bioscience, Biotechnology, and Biochemistry*, U.S. National Library of Medicine, Dec. 2008, www.ncbi.nlm.nih.gov/pubmed/19060399.

Jiang, Xiaojing, et al. "Lipids and Cholesterol-Lowering Activity of Red Cabbage Microgreens." *The FASEB Journal*, 1 Apr. 2016, www.fasebj.org/doi/abs/10.1096/fasebj.30.1_supplement.431.8.

Jiang, Yu, et al. "Cruciferous Vegetable Intake Is Inversely Correlated with Circulating Levels of Proinflammatory Markers in Women." *Journal of the Academy of Nutrition and Dietetics*, U.S. National Library of Medicine, May 2014, www.ncbi.nlm.nih.gov/pubmed/24630682.

Kim, Jae Kwang, and Sang Un Park. "Current Potential Health Benefits of Sulforaphane." *EXCLI Journal*, Leibniz Research Centre for Working Environment and Human Factors, 13 Oct. 2016, www.ncbi.nlm.nih.gov/pmc/articles/PMC5225737/.

Lam, Kim, et al. "Cruciferous Vegetable Consumption and Lung Cancer Risk: A Systematic Review." *Cancer Epidemiology, Biomarkers & Prevention*, American Association for Cancer Research, 1 Jan. 2009, cebp.aacrjournals.org/content/18/1/184.

Lattimer, James M, and Mark D Haub. "Effects of Dietary Fiber and Its Components on Metabolic Health." *Nutrients*, MDPI, Dec. 2010, www.ncbi.nlm.nih.gov/pmc/articles/PMC3257631/.

Lee, Cho J. "Flaxseed Sprouts Induce Apoptosis and Inhibit Growth in MCF-7 and MDA-MB-231 Human Breast Cancer Cells." *In Vitro Cellular & Developmental Biology - Animal*, Springer-Verlag, 1 Jan. 1970, link.springer.com/article/10.1007/s11626-012-9492-1#citeas.

Li, Min, et al. "Fruit and Vegetable Intake and Risk of Type 2 Diabetes Mellitus: Meta-Analysis of Prospective Cohort Studies." *BMJ Open*, BMJ Publishing Group, 5 Nov. 2014, www.ncbi.nlm.nih.gov/pubmed/25377009/.

Lin, Long-Ze, and James M Harnly. "Phenolic Component Profiles of Mustard Greens, Yu Choy, and 15 Other Brassica Vegetables." *Journal of Agricultural and Food Chemistry*, U.S. National Library of Medicine, 9 June 2010, www.ncbi.nlm.nih.gov/pubmed/20465307.

"Lutein & Zeaxanthin." *American Optometric Association*, www.aoa.org/patients-and-public/caring-for-your-vision/diet-and-nutrition/lutein.

Malar, D Sheeja, and K Pandima Devi. "Dietary Polyphenols for Treatment of Alzheimer's Disease--Future Research and Development." *Current Pharmaceutical Biotechnology*, U.S. National Library of Medicine, 2014, www.ncbi.nlm.nih.gov/pubmed/25312617.

Malar, D Sheeja, and K Pandima Devi. "Dietary Polyphenols for Treatment of Alzheimer's Disease--Future Research and Development." *Current Pharmaceutical Biotechnology*, U.S. National Library of Medicine, 2014, www.ncbi.nlm.nih.gov/pubmed/25312617.

Pasko, Pawel, et al. "Rutabaga (Brassica Napus L. Var. Napobrassica) Seeds, Roots, and Sprouts: a Novel Kind of Food with Antioxidant Properties and Proapoptotic Potential in Hep G2 Hepatoma Cell Line." *Journal of Medicinal Food*, U.S. National Library of Medicine, Aug. 2013, www.ncbi.nlm.nih.gov/pubmed/23957358.

"Red Cabbage Microgreens Could Reduce Risk of Cardiovascular Disease." *Medical News Today*, MediLexicon International, www.medicalnewstoday.com/articles/314793#Microgreens-reduced-circulating-LDL-cholesterol-in-mice-fed-high-fat-diet.

Sarkar, Fazlul H, and Yiwei Li. "Soy Isoflavones and Cancer Prevention." *Cancer Investigation*, U.S. National Library of Medicine, 2003, www.ncbi.nlm.nih.gov/pubmed/14628433/.

"Sensitivity to Bitter Tastes May Be Why Some People Eat Fewer Vegetables." *ScienceDaily*, ScienceDaily, 11 Nov. 2019, www.sciencedaily.com/releases/2019/11/191111084916.htm.

Sun, Jianghao, et al. "Profiling Polyphenols in Five Brassica Species Microgreens by UHPLC-PDA-ESI/HRMS(n.)." *Journal of Agricultural and Food Chemistry*, U.S. National Library of Medicine, 20 Nov. 2013, www.ncbi.nlm.nih.gov/pmc/articles/PMC3915300/.

Sun, Jianghao, et al. "Profiling Polyphenols in Five Brassica Species Microgreens by UHPLC-PDA-ESI/HRMS(n.)." *Journal of Agricultural and Food Chemistry*, U.S. National Library of Medicine, 20 Nov. 2013, www.ncbi.nlm.nih.gov/pmc/articles/PMC3915300/.

Tangney, Christy C, and Heather E Rasmussen. "Polyphenols, Inflammation, and Cardiovascular Disease." *Current Atherosclerosis Reports*, U.S. National Library of Medicine, May 2013, www.ncbi.nlm.nih.gov/pmc/articles/PMC3651847/.

Turati, Federica, et al. "Fruit and Vegetables and Cancer Risk: a Review of Southern European Studies." *The British Journal of Nutrition*, U.S. National Library of Medicine, Apr. 2015, www.ncbi.nlm.nih.gov/pubmed/26148912.

Warner, Jennifer. "Tiny Microgreens Packed With Nutrients." *WebMD*, WebMD, 31 Aug. 2012, www.webmd.com/diet/news/20120831/tiny-microgreens-packed-nutrients#1.

Weber, Carolyn F. "Broccoli Microgreens: A Mineral-Rich Crop That Can Diversify Food Systems." *Frontiers in Nutrition*, Frontiers Media S.A., 23 Mar. 2017, www.ncbi.nlm.nih.gov/pmc/articles/PMC5362588/.

Xiao, Zhenlei, et al. "Assessment of Vitamin and Carotenoid Concentrations of Emerging Food Products: Edible Microgreens." *Journal of Agricultural and Food Chemistry*, U.S. National Library of Medicine, 8 Aug. 2012, www.ncbi.nlm.nih.gov/pubmed/22812633/.

Xiao, Zhenlei, et al. "Assessment of Vitamin and Carotenoid Concentrations of Emerging Food Products: Edible Microgreens." *Journal of Agricultural and Food Chemistry*, U.S. National Library of Medicine, 8 Aug. 2012, www.ncbi.nlm.nih.gov/pubmed/22812633/.

Xiao, Zhenlei, et al. "Effect of Light Exposure on Sensorial Quality, Concentrations of Bioactive Compounds and Antioxidant Capacity of Radish Microgreens during Low Temperature Storage." *Food Chemistry*, U.S. National Library of Medicine, 15 May 2014, www.ncbi.nlm.nih.gov/pubmed/24423559.

Xiao, Zhenlei, et al. "Microgreens of Brassicaceae: Mineral Composition and Content of 30 Varieties." *Journal of Food Composition and Analysis*, Academic Press, 22 Apr. 2016, www.sciencedirect.com/science/article/abs/pii/S0889157516300448.